CW01465456

Living in Laodicea

A call to repentance from compromise with the world

Peter H. Noble

New Wine Press

New Wine Press
PO Box 17
Chichester
England PO20 6YB

Copyright © 2002 Peter H. Noble

All rights reserved. No part of this publication may be reproduced, stored in a retrieval system, or transmitted in any form or by any means, electronic, mechanical, photocopying or otherwise, without the prior written consent of the publisher. Short extracts may be used for review purposes.

All Scripture quotations are taken from the Revised Standard Version, copyright © 1952 and 1971

ISBN: 1 903725 12 7

Typeset by CRB Associates, Reepham, Norfolk.
Printed in England by Clays Ltd, St Ives plc.

The sum of Thy word is truth;
and every one of Thy righteous
ordinances endures for ever.
(Psalm 119:160)

*This book is written
for those who love the Lord
and His Church,
and is
dedicated to
my wife, Margaret,
a true support and helpmate.*

*Every attempt has been made
to clear all copyright permissions,
and acknowledge all sources.
Any omissions will be included
in subsequent editions.*

Contents

Preface

This book is about compromise and repentance.

It is the conviction of the author that the Christian Church in western countries is riddled with compromise. We have largely abandoned the faith once delivered to the saints, and replaced it with secular standards and aspirations. Instead of following the Lord, we are trailing the coat-tails of the world.

As such we stand in the same position as the church in Laodicea, which is portrayed for our warning and benefit in the book of Revelation.

Our concessions to the spirit of the age are extremely serious. They are leading us far from the truth, and making us infinitely less capable of proclaiming the everlasting gospel. Instead of a life-changing message which challenges the attitudes of the world, we are presenting a tawdry and powerless religion which can affect nothing.

Yet Jesus loves His Church. We are, after all, His Body. So He calls us to return to Him in repentance, and walk once more in the truth of His ways. I pray that all who read this book may be encouraged to offer such repentance, for it is through true contrition that the Lord acts in sovereign power for the good of His people, and to the glory of His name.

Peter Noble

PART ONE

LAODICEA THEN

Chapter 1

The Trouble with Laodicea

A whimsey, based on fact

The time: 94 AD.

The place: Laodicea – a prosperous city in the Roman
province of Asia.

According to its own estimation the church in Laodicea was
doing well.

The church coffers were full. Even the treasurer was happy.
It was not that the members gave liberally. They had no need
to. The church did not need much, as there was no building to
maintain. They met in the home of Alexander, a wealthy
banker. In the early days they had used the house of an old
lady called Nympha, but when Alexander offered his home, it
was agreed by a large majority that they should accept. After
all, his residence was much grander, and it gave the church
some standing in the community.

They had offered to pay Alexander for the use of his home,
or a room at the back to be more accurate, but he had always
refused.

'Accept it as my giving', he said.

What a wise and careful man was Alexander.

The church was not small. Altogether there were one
hundred and fifty members, but hardly anyone came on a

regular weekly basis, and Alexander only appeared now and again. There were so many other things to do. Business was booming, and that demanded attention. The weather was glorious for most of the year, and trips to the countryside were very popular. And, above all, there was the hospitality. Everyone was so friendly. It was parties every week, with enough wine to satisfy even the hardest drinker. Unfortunately many get-togethers were held on Sundays, but surely the Lord understood. What would the world think of Christians who refused invitations to parties? It would have been a very bad witness. One or two older church members were not happy about the things that went on at these festivities, but the church leadership now taught that self-expression was essential for human development.

It was a shame that the services were not better attended, but still, thirty or so was not too bad. It was far more than the folks in Philadelphia could muster, and at least there were no troubles in Laodicea. Some churches in Asia had great upsets. They were always quarrelling over doctrine. One group would say one thing, another the opposite. Rumour had it that the churches in Ephesus and Pergamum were split apart. It was even worse at Thyatira, where one member claimed to be a prophetess and was running her own fellowship group.

'You will find nothing like that in Laodicea', said Lapidodorus, the chief deacon. 'All that theology. As if it mattered anyway. Surely all roads lead to God? He doesn't worry about what people believe, just so long as they believe something. Let each think as he will, and we can all be friends.'

'Some churches,' he continued, 'are even being persecuted by outsiders. Those poor folk in Smyrna, for example. Such nice people. But so bigoted. We can't tell what they are playing at. How did they get into that state? If only they had kept a low profile, it would never have happened.

'We have found that a little compromise here, a small shift of emphasis there, and we are accepted by everyone in the city. Only the other week, our angel, that's our leader, was invited to our world famous Medical School to present the diplomas.

'We heard all about it in his sermon the following Sunday. He told us that there had been a bit of mumbo-jumbo at first, to Asclepius the god of healing, and to another god called Men. Afterwards they had a slap-up meal, with all sorts of fresh meats, which had been sacrificed in the temple of Asclepius just before the prize-giving. He said we should not criticise the world, but meet it on its own terms, and become involved in the life of our city.

'This led us to invite the high priest of Asclepius to preach at our harvest festival in three weeks time. He will surely have some new insights for us, for no religion has all the truth. In fact we went further and invited the Dean of the Medical School as well. We may get a few more in the congregation that day, perhaps some students from the college.

'Yes, on the whole, the church is doing very well. Our city fathers always tell us that a large bank balance is a sign of success, and the key to all happiness. We agree.

'To be frank, there was a spot of trouble a year or two ago. The old Apostle John, who lived in Ephesus, paid us a visit. He said some very nasty things, and upset us all. He was always going on about the world being evil, and that we should be different from the world. What nonsense! We are in the world, and we must be part of it. Does he want us all to go and live on a desert island?

'Talking about desert islands, that is where he is at the moment. He overstepped the mark a year or so ago, and upset our Roman Governor. So off John went to Patmos. Poor old man. That will keep him quiet.

'Now we just live as we want, at peace with everybody. We have no troubles inside or outside the church, and we know we shall go to heaven when we die. We mix with the world, enjoy the things of this life and let others do the same. How good is God. How pleased He must be with our church.

'Yes, God is pleased with us. If He could speak to us, He would tell us so.

'What's this? . . . a letter? . . . To the angel? . . . From Jesus? . . . What does it say?'

To the angel of the church in Laodicea write:

The words of the Amen, the faithful and true witness, the beginning of God's creation.

I know your works: you are neither cold nor hot. Would that you were cold or hot! So, because you are lukewarm, and neither cold nor hot, I will spew you out of my mouth.

For you say, I am rich, I have prospered, and I need nothing; not knowing that you are wretched, pitiable, poor, blind, and naked.

Therefore I counsel you to buy from me gold refined by fire, that you may be rich, and white garments to clothe you and keep the shame of your nakedness from being seen, and salve to anoint your eyes, that you may see.

Those whom I love, I reprove and chasten; so be zealous and repent.

Behold, I stand at the door and knock; if any one hears my voice and opens the door, I will come in to him and eat with him, and he with Me.

He who conquers, I will grant him to sit with Me on My throne, as I Myself conquered and sat down with My Father on His throne.

He who has an ear, let him hear what the Spirit says to the churches.

Chapter 2

Laodicea: the City

'A most distinguished city'
(Pliny)

Laodicea was a city halfway up a valley in what we know
today as Turkey. It shared its valley with two other cities.
Hierapolis was six miles away, up in the hills, and Colossae
lay downhill on the banks of the river Lycus, ten miles from
Laodicea.

A Greek king, Antiochus of Syria, built Laodicea in 250 BC,
and named it after his wife, Laodice. It was intended to be a
fortress, but that plan came to nothing because the city water
supply was carried by aqueducts from hot springs near
Hierapolis, and could easily be cut.

Laodicea fell to various armies over the years, and was
finally captured by the Romans in 133 BC. They made it a
centre of government. From then on the city prospered, and
by New Testament times it was fabulously rich. As well as
being one of the most important financial centres of the
world, it had a thriving woollen industry and a world famous
medical school which also manufactured pharmaceuticals.

Many inhabitants were very wealthy, and the good
climate, along with vineyards which produced high quality
wines, attracted the affluent from all over the Mediterranean.
Pliny, a Roman who lived in the first century AD, described
Laodicea as a most distinguished city, but it also had the

reputation of being a proud, self-reliant and ostentatious place, where money and position ruled.

The one fly in the ointment was that the whole region was especially vulnerable to earthquakes. In 60 AD a strong quake destroyed Laodicea and other neighbouring cities. The central government offered financial aid, but unlike the rest of the area the Laodiceans refused to accept it. They declared they would pay for their reconstruction out of their own pockets, and to the amazement of all they did just that. The Roman historian, Tacitus, wrote that:

> 'Laodicea, one of the famous Asiatic cities, was laid in ruins by an earthquake, but recovered by its own resources, without assistance from ourselves.'[1]

Such were the riches and the pride of this most distinguished city, and it was into this opulent, smug, pleasure-loving world that the Laodicean church was born.

Reference

1. Tacitus, *Annals* 14.27, trans. John Jackson, William Heinemann, 1981, p. 151.

Chapter 3

Laodicea: the Church

*'We have heard of your faith in Christ Jesus and
of the love which you have for all the saints.'*
(Colossians 1:4)

'You are lukewarm.'
(Revelation 3:16)

I

The gospel was first brought to the cities of the Lycus valley
by a Christian named Epaphras. In his letter to the church in
Colossae, written around 60 AD, Paul reminded his readers
how they first heard the gospel *'from Epaphras our beloved
fellow servant'* (Colossians 1:7), and how he *'has worked hard
for you and for those in Laodicea and in Hierapolis'* (Colossians
4:13). In common with other churches, the Laodicean
Christians met in private houses (Colossians 4:15).

Paul wrote a letter to the Laodicean church. This was
delivered at the same time as one to Colossae. He told the
Colossian Christians,

> *'When this letter has been read among you, have it read also
> in the church of the Laodiceans; and see that you read
> also the letter from Laodicea.'* (Colossians 4:16)

There is no surviving copy of the letter to Laodicea.

From Paul's letter to Colossae, we can infer that the Laodicean church was in good spiritual condition.

False teachers had infiltrated the Colossian church, and were teaching that faith in Jesus was not sufficient for salvation. They said various observances such as circumcision, fasting, and worship of angels, were necessary in order to achieve heaven. Paul's insistence on an exchange of letters suggests that the same heresy had penetrated Laodicea. Thus we can infer that the Laodicean church was alive, for the devil only attacks strong churches.

Paul also said the Colossian Christians were *'established in the faith'*, and *'abounding in thanksgiving'* (Colossians 2:7). They had a *'love in the Spirit'* (Colossians 1:8) which expressed itself in love *'for all the saints'* (Colossians 1:4). Since letters had to be exchanged, and both churches had been founded and taught by the same man, there is no doubt that the same vibrant faith was found in Laodicea. This is only to be expected, as church members were people who had been converted to Christ from paganism. They would know the difference between the old life and the new.

II

Things, however, did not stay that way. Within thirty years, the Laodicean church had degenerated to a shadow of its former self. This is shown in the letter Jesus sent to the church.[1] Originally this letter was given to the apostle John, who was in exile on the island of Patmos, and is part of the great vision known to us as the **Revelation to John**.

Jesus exposed two problems which were afflicting His Church in Laodicea.

The first was lukewarmness.

> *'You are neither cold nor hot ... you are lukewarm.'*
> (Revelation 3:15, 16)

The word 'cold' means 'freezing cold', and the word 'hot' means 'boiling hot'. These Christians were neither zealous for Jesus, nor against Him. They were like their water supply, which was very hot when it came out of the ground near Hierapolis, but tepid by the time it reached Laodicea.

Underneath the lukewarmness of the church lay a deeper problem. The Laodicean Christians had compromised with the affluent world in which they lived. Jesus said of them,

> *'You say, I am rich, I have prospered, and I need nothing.'*
> (Revelation 3:17)

The Christians had fallen into the trap of emulating the materialism and love of money which was a hallmark of the wider community. The citizens of Laodicea trusted in their wealth, and the church was doing the same. Instead of challenging the world around it, these Christians had absorbed its standards.

It cannot be stressed too strongly that this compromise was the basic problem of the Laodicean church. It was because they had adopted the values of the world that they had become lukewarm in their Christian life. Compromise with the world came first, and lukewarmness naturally followed on. Jesus showed this link when He said,

> *'You are neither hot nor cold ... For you say I am rich...'*
> (Revelation 3:15, 17)

Reference

1. Revelation 3:14–22.

Chapter 4

Laodicea: the Road to Disaster

*'The gate is wide and the way is easy, that leads to destruction,
and those who enter by it are many.'*
(Matthew 7:13)

I

The Laodicean church was heading towards total disaster.
Compromise and the consequent lukewarmness were only
the first signs of decline. Other symptoms would inevitably
follow.

A compromising church always becomes corrupted by false
beliefs, for absolute biblical truths are abhorrent to tepid
Christians. Such a church also hates evangelism. When a
church adjusts to the world it sees no reason to change
things. Rather it develops a universalist theory which holds
that everyone will ultimately be saved.

Similarly, half-hearted Christians will not strive after moral
perfection. Nor are they too concerned about the way others
live. They will not attempt to bring God's purity to a fallen
generation, but will adopt the standards of the day.

Lukewarmness also affects the inner spiritual life. There is
no perceived need to read and study the Scriptures, and no
necessity to pray, except in an emergency, or in a church
service. Accommodating Christians give an outward show of

their religion, but it is powerless and hollow, having no value in the eyes of God nor in the lives of men.

Spiritual blindness is an inevitable result of compromise. Those so afflicted cannot repent of their sins, for they do not see them. Thus they come to think that they have achieved full spiritual stature. This in turn engenders pride, leading to criticism of 'imperfect' Christians. The final result is broken relationships, and the 'perfect' Christians become hard, fault-finding and unhappy people.

Compromise leads the church to measure its success by secular standards. If the world holds that large majorities are a sign of achievement, then the church looks for big congregations, and worries little about the quality of Christian life. On the other hand if wealth is a measure of having arrived, the church rejoices in a large bank balance and develops a prosperity theology which explicitly links earthly riches with God's blessing. This leads to pride in those who pass the test, and hopeless despair in those who do not.

An insidious outcome of compromise is peace with the world. When a church conforms to its surroundings it loses its cutting edge, and does nothing to which the world would object. The world then embraces the church, holding it in a deadly grip. This spells serious trouble, for as Jesus said,

> *'Woe to you, when all men speak well of you, for so their fathers did to the false prophets.'* (Luke 6:26)

II

We are not told exactly how far the Laodicean compromise had developed, but we can see some indications of the church's regression.

As well as being afflicted by lukewarmness, the church was filled with pride, for it said, *'I need nothing'* (Revelation 3:17). Only the proud dare say this. The humble man knows that no good dwells in him, and that he constantly needs the grace and power of God.

The church in Laodicea faced no persecution. This is a remarkable fact, since at that time the Church as a whole was suffering from official state oppression. The Laodiceans had obviously conformed sufficiently for the world to leave them alone.

By a similar token the church was no longer troubled by false teachers. Unlike the first Christians in Laodicea, the second generation of believers clearly posed no threat to the powers of darkness.

The full gravity of the situation is shown by the fact that Jesus found nothing good to say about the church. As well as giving the apostle John a letter for Laodicea, Jesus gave him letters for six other churches (Revelation 2:1–3:13). In His description of these six churches, Jesus found something good to say about each of them. But Laodicea was bad news from beginning to end. This church, set in a fine and affluent area, had nothing that was pleasing to its Lord. It was well clothed with the riches of this world, but threadbare as regards the treasures of heaven.

Yet the Laodicean church had not reached the end, otherwise Jesus would not have spoken in the way He did. They were in great danger, but there was still time to win them back.

Chapter 5

Laodicea:
the Way Forward

'Be zealous and repent.'
(Revelation 3:19)

I

In spite of all their failings Jesus loved the Laodiceans and this love shines throughout His letter. Central to everything are the words,

> *'Those whom I love, I reprove and chasten; so be zealous and repent.'*   (Revelation 3:19)

It is impossible to over-emphasise this verse. Jesus was not speaking in anger but in tones of pure love. Neither was He speaking in despair, as if there was no solution to the problem of compromise. Things could be changed, but only if the Laodiceans repented and returned to their Lord.

Therefore all through His letter, Jesus lovingly encouraged His people to repent.

II

First He warned them of the result of their compromise.

> *'Because you are lukewarm, and neither cold nor hot, I will spew you out of my mouth.'*   (Revelation 3:16)

One can imagine the well-heeled, urbane Laodiceans cringing with horror at these words and all that they implied.

Yet here is love. Jesus was not saying He was going to be rid of the Laodicean church then and there. The words *'I will'* implied no time scale, either short or long. The Laodiceans were being given time to repent, but they could not sit back and put things off, for the situation was desperate.

III

Jesus continued by describing the spiritual condition of the church. He said,

> *'You are wretched, pitiable, poor, blind and naked.'*
> (Revelation 3:17)

All the worldly pride and arrogance in which the Laodicean Christians were wrapped was stripped away, and they were exposed as spiritually impoverished. In His original words, Jesus emphasised the *'you'* and put *'the'* in front of wretched. He said in effect, *'You above all others are the wretched ones. There is nobody as bad as you.'*

Here again is love. Before they could repent the Laodiceans had to be aware of their true standing before the Lord. It was doing them no favours to say things were going well, when the church was collapsing about itself.

Further, within these strong words there is a pointer to the way back. The word *'pitiable'* means standing in need of mercy. Jesus showed that only the mercy and the grace of

God could save the Laodiceans. They could not rely on riches or their position in the world.

IV

After this onslaught Jesus spoke tenderly to His people, and assured them that God was merciful, and His grace freely available.

> *'Therefore I counsel you to buy from me gold refined by fire, that you may be rich, and white garments to clothe you and to keep the shame of your nakedness from being seen, and salve to anoint your eyes, that you may see.'*
>
> (Revelation 3:18)

Gold, garments and salve were the life blood of the Laodicean economy. Yet Jesus was not talking about earthly gold, clothing or salve. The gold refined by fire represented true spiritual riches, the *'treasure in the heavens that does not fail'* (Luke 12:33). In direct contrast to clothes made of black wool for which Laodicea was famous, the white garments signified sins forgiven and washed away. Eye salve was a best selling product of the medical school, but the salve of which Jesus spoke symbolised His healing light. He was offering spiritual light to the Laodiceans who once could see but now were blind.

He said,

> *'I counsel you to buy from me.'*   (Revelation 3:18)

He alone was the source of all these blessings. The Laodiceans could not give gold coinage for them. They could only be bought *'without money and without price'* (Isaiah 55:1), that is by faith and repentance.

V

Jesus' love flowed in full spate as He continued,

> *'Behold, I stand at the door and knock; if any one hears my voice and opens the door, I will come in to him and eat with him, and he with me.'*   (Revelation 3:20)

This was a direct personal appeal to each individual. Previously Jesus had spoken to the church as a whole, but now He said, *'If any one hears my voice.'* Every single member of the Laodicean church was of the greatest importance to the Lord.

Jesus did not force Himself on anyone, but stood and waited for a response. The Laodiceans had to decide for themselves whether or not to accept His love.

VI

Jesus undergirded His appeal with three promises.

The first was a pledge to accept the repentance of all who turned to Him.

> *'If any one hears my voice and opens the door, I will come in to him.'*   (Revelation 3:20)

The second promise is found in the words *'I will ... eat with him, and he with me'* (Revelation 3:20). In those days a meal was an occasion where people took time to enjoy one another's company in an atmosphere of complete acceptance. So Jesus promised total forgiveness and deep fellowship with each Laodicean who repented.

Finally Jesus gave the assurance,

> *'He who conquers, I will grant him to sit with me on my throne, as I myself conquered and sat down with my Father on His throne.'*   (Revelation 3:21)

The lukewarm Laodiceans were promised great and eternal glory, but the path to that glory lay through the cross. Only by renouncing the world, and seeking the things that are above could such blessings be attained.

VII

Jesus ended His message with an urgent plea to His people to listen. He did not want His words to fall on deaf ears. Such was His persistent love towards His compromising church.

> *'He who has an ear, let him hear what the Spirit says to the churches.'*   (Revelation 3:22)

All that was necessary had now been said. The choice confronting the Laodiceans was well defined. Either they repented, and were restored to fellowship with Jesus, or they continued as they were and faced expulsion from the Body of Christ.

Did the Laodiceans repent? Only the Lord knows. Of greater importance to us is the eternal truth of this message. Whenever a church is entangled with the world, there is only one way forward, and that is repentance. He who has an ear, let him hear.

PART TWO

LAODICEA NOW

Chapter 6

The One Body

'If one member suffers, all suffer together;
if one member is honoured, all rejoice together.'
(1 Corinthians 12:26)

I

In the second part of this book we will consider six specific areas of compromise, which show how the Laodicean spirit is alive and flourishing in today's Church.

Before we embark on this course, let us heed a word of warning. When we say that the Church has compromised, we are confessing that **we** have compromised. The sin of the Church is **our** sin.

We are not bemoaning the Laodicean attitude of church leaders only, for we are all involved. Every one of us stands convicted in the sight of God. This truth holds even though most of the illustrations of compromise are statements and actions of individual church leaders or groups. Such examples must be chosen because they are openly and widely reported.

In a similar vein we are not talking about the failings of just one branch of the Church. Many examples of the spirit of Laodicea which appear in the following chapters have been drawn from the Anglican Church. This in no way implies that this church is worse than any other, for that is not the case, and, indeed, there are many fine congregations within the Church of England, as there are in all other Christian denominations in our land. It is merely that the author was a serving clergyman in the Church of England, and is more keenly aware of the situation within that part of the Body of Christ.

Paul told the Corinthian Christians,

> *'You are the body of Christ, and individually members of it.'*
> (1 Corinthians 12:27)

He also taught the Christians in Rome that,

> *'...we, though many, are one body in Christ, and individually members one of another.'* (Romans 12:5)

All Christians, not just those in Corinth and Rome, are deeply united in Christ. We are individuals, with our own personalities, weaknesses and strengths. Yet we are part of the same body, joined together through our Lord. Therefore when one part of the body sins, the whole body is tainted.

We do not say of a shoplifter, 'His hands are thieves.' We say, 'He is a thief'. His whole body and personality is involved in what his hands have done. So it is in the Church. We cannot say, 'The Anglicans have compromised in one issue, and the Methodists have gone astray in another.' Rather we must say, 'We have compromised on both issues.'

When Daniel, who lived in exile in Babylon, was made aware that seventy years must pass before the end of the desolation of Jerusalem, he turned to the Lord in repentance. He was well aware that the sins of his forbears caused the fall of Jerusalem, but he always included himself amongst those who had sinned. He said *'we have sinned'* (Daniel 9:5), *'we have not listened to thy servants the prophets'* (Daniel 9:6). He never said *'They have sinned'*. In fact, Daniel described his prayer as *'confessing my sin and the sin of my people Israel'* (Daniel 9:20).

We must never allow the sad condition of the Church to become an occasion for pride. As with Daniel, it should become a means towards an acknowledgement of our personal sins, and lead us to repentance.

II

Sinful compromise starts almost unseen, and develops slowly over a number of years, or even over centuries. A full-blown compromise, involving the denial of a particular Christian truth, would not initially be accepted by most Christians. It has to move slowly, eating away at the traditional belief bit by bit, working for a small modification here, or an exception there. This is known by some as the drip-feed tactic, and it has been remarkably successful in many areas of Church life. The results are only seen towards the end of the process, when the perversion of truth has been well discussed in a non-judgemental manner. By that time, most church members have become so conditioned that the total compromise is accepted without question.

Often a particular compromise is first broached in academic theological writings, where the authors claim freedom of thought. Although very few people read these works, they are the conduit by which the compromise spreads into theological colleges and more popular writings. From thence it reaches the pulpit and the general teaching ministry of the Church.

Three services which were a triumphant and open statement of the liberal gospel of compromise have taken place in English cathedrals since the mid-1980s. The first was the consecration, in York Minster, of Dr David Jenkins as Bishop of Durham in July 1984. The second was the World Wide Fund for Nature's interfaith service in Canterbury Cathedral in September 1989, and the third the Lesbian and Gay Christian Movement's 20th anniversary service in Southwark Cathedral in November 1996.

These gatherings did not appear out of the blue. Behind them lay much talking, thinking and writing. Many generations of church leaders, writers and theologians had argued that it was permissible to disbelieve various doctrines of the Church and still remain within the fold, even to the extent of holding positions of leadership. Similarly the lie that Christianity is not a unique religion had been slowly disseminating through the Church for many years, as had the deceit that a sexual act which God calls an abomination is now acceptable.

The one good thing about these services is that they show how far the spirit of Laodicea has eaten its way into the Body of Christ. We cannot say that compromise is not happening, for it is placarded before us in all its horror.

SCRIPTURE

Chapter 7

Where Truth is Found

'Thy word is truth.'
(John 17:17)

The Bible is the bedrock of the Church. The Christian faith
in all its fullness is found in the pages of Holy Scripture.
From the beginning of Genesis to the end of Revelation we
have the truth about God, given to us from God Himself.

Paul wrote,

'All scripture is inspired by God.' (2 Timothy 3:16)

By 'scripture', Paul meant the Old Testament, although the
New Testament was in the process of being compiled, and
parts were already accepted as scripture.[1]

The phrase *'inspired by God'* literally means *'God-breathed'*,
and describes how the Bible came to be written. The Holy
Spirit, the breath of God, influenced the different writers of
the books of the Bible, and ensured that what they wrote was
accurate and dependable.

By using the word *'all'*, Paul makes it clear that this truth
applies to the whole Bible. We cannot say that some parts are
inspired and others are not. Every book in every detail is truly
the Word of God.

The apostle Peter said exactly the same in his second letter.

*'First of all you must understand this, that no prophecy of
scripture is a matter of one's own interpretation, because no*

*prophecy ever came by the impulse of man, but men moved
by the Holy Spirit spoke from God.'* (2 Peter 1:20, 21)

The word 'moved' is a nautical term which speaks of a
sailing boat being driven by the wind. In a similar way, the
Holy Spirit carried men along, giving them power and
direction to write down the words of God. The authors were
not mere machines who took down the message by dictation,
but they were open to the direction of the Holy Spirit as the
sails of a boat are open to the wind. Thus we cannot give our
own interpretation to the Scriptures. We must humbly read,
hear and obey what God says.

Peter and Paul were, of course, following in the footsteps of
Jesus, who by His teaching and use of the Scriptures, showed
the Old Testament was the reliable and trustworthy Word of
God.

When quoting Psalm 110:1, Jesus said it was written
by *'David ... inspired by the Holy Spirit'* (Mark 12:36). On
another occasion He quoted Psalm 82:6, and described it as
'the word of God', adding *'scripture cannot be broken'* (John
10:34, 35).

Jesus' use of scripture was consistent with His teaching. He
overcame His temptations in the wilderness by quoting three
verses from Deuteronomy, prefacing each with the words,
'It is written' (Matthew 4:4, 7, 10). When the Sadducees tried
to catch Him out with a trick question about one bride for
seven brothers, Jesus answered them from the Scriptures
(Mark 12:18–27). The Word of God had power to overcome
evil, and was the final arbiter in all matters of belief.

Jesus clearly regarded the Old Testament as historically
accurate. He mentioned Jonah being swallowed by the fish,
Noah's flood, and Lot escaping from Sodom as factual
occurrences (Matthew 12:39–41; Luke 17:26–27; 17:28–32).

Before His death, Jesus said to His apostles,

*'The Counsellor, the Holy Spirit, whom the Father will send
in my name, he will teach you all things, and bring to your
remembrance all that I have said to you.'* (John 14:26)

After Pentecost, under the direction of the Spirit, the apostles taught about Jesus. Some of His sayings and deeds were written down, and became part of the new scriptures, the new Spirit-filled Word of God.

The Scriptures can be trusted. God does not lie or make mistakes. His Word is our guide to true belief and godly living. As Paul puts it,

> *'All scripture is ... profitable for teaching, for reproof, for correction, and for training in righteousness, that the man of God may be complete, equipped for every good work.'*
> (2 Timothy 3:16, 17)

The Bible is not just another book, which can be read and judged as a human creation. We cannot stand over it, and remove or alter passages which contradict the world's current thinking and standards. That would be passing judgement on God Himself.

This trust in the Bible as God's Word has been normative for all Christians down the ages.

For instance, Athanasius, who was bishop of Alexandria in the 4th century taught that 'the sacred and inspired Scriptures are sufficient in themselves to declare the truth.'[2]

In a more pastoral vein, Boniface, the 8th century English missionary, spoke of the Bible in words reminiscent of those of Peter,

> 'Can there be a more fitting pursuit in youth or a more valuable possession in old age than a knowledge of Holy Writ? In the midst of storms it will preserve you from the dangers of shipwreck and guide you to the shore of an enchanting paradise and the everlasting bliss of the angels.'[3]

Article 6 of the Church of England, written in the 16th century, puts it in different language, but with the same meaning:

'Holy Scripture containeth all things necessary to salvation: so that whatsoever is not read therein, nor may be proved thereby, is not to be required of any man, that it should be believed as an article of the faith, or be thought requisite or necessary to salvation.'[4]

Armed with an accurate and inerrant Bible, the Church had a powerful weapon in its fight against heresy and compromise. This is why the post-apostolic church spent so much time and prayer in defining the books of the New Testament.

Therefore before a Laodicean compromise can take hold in the Church, the authority of the Bible has to be undermined. It is only as the Word of God is explained away, or treated as out of date and irrelevant, that the way is open for accommodation with the world.

References

1. 2 Peter 3:15, 16, where Paul's letters are described as scripture.
2. Athanasius, Adv. Gentes 1.3. *Nicene and Post-Nicene Fathers of the Christian Church*, ed. H. Wace and P. Schaff, Oxford, 1892, p. 4.
3. Boniface, 'Letter to Nithard', 716–719, *The Anglo-Saxon Missionaries in Germany*, trans. C.H. Talbot, Sheed and Ward, 1954, p. 66.
4. Of the Sufficiency of the Scriptures, Article 6, Articles of Religion, *The Book of Common Prayer*.

Chapter 8

The Subversion of the Word of God

'Cursed is the man who trusts in man and makes flesh his arm,
*whose heart turns away from the L*ORD*.'*
(Jeremiah 17:5)

I

The last two to three hundred years have seen a sustained attack on the veracity of the Bible. It has been alleged that the Scriptures are not consonant with modern knowledge, and therefore must be adjusted or discarded.

The roots of this compromise are found in the late 17th and early 18th centuries, when influential European thinkers sought to subject everything, including Christianity, to the rule of reason. If something could not be justified rationally, it had to be discarded. Thus the Scottish philosopher David Hume (1711–1776) denied the possibility of miracles. He held it was unreasonable to believe in miracles because the uniform course of nature cannot be interrupted. On such grounds many treated the miracles of both the Old and the New Testaments as untrue.

Rationalism also invaded the Church. Some clergy and theologians subjected Scripture to the dictates of reason, and anything that appeared unreasonable, including miracles, the virgin birth and the resurrection of Jesus, was reinterpreted or jettisoned.

The rise of modern science in the 18th and 19th centuries led men to look for empirical proof of all truths, including the tenets of Christianity. If such could not be obtained, then Christian beliefs had to be set aside. Worldly tools were thus used to dismantle the Word of God.

The motives of some who compromised in this way were honourable. They wanted to make the Christian faith accessible to modern man, and argued that if the Bible could be reinterpreted according to the thought of the day, modern thinkers would be attracted to Christ and His teachings. Sadly this view was mistaken, as the history of the decline of Christianity in the western democracies has shown. The truth is that men of any age will never be drawn towards a watered-down religion.

Although many churchfolk reacted against this worldly view, the rejection of the literal truth of the Bible gathered pace. The advent of Darwinism was an important staging post and catalyst in this process.

The general acceptance of Darwin's views on evolution, which were first published in 1859, put Christians in a dilemma. They realised that Darwin's teachings were diametrically opposed to the traditional biblical understanding of creation. The first two chapters of Genesis teach that each species was created separately, and the whole act of creation took place in the very short time of six days. Darwin, on the other hand, postulated an evolutionary model, whereby the species evolved by natural selection, which of necessity required millions of years.

Some resolved this dilemma by abandoning Genesis altogether. Others said the chapters were not a historical account of creation, but a parable or a myth, which could be modified to fit Darwin's ideas. Various theories to harmonise religion and science, all of which compromised the literal truth of Genesis, were proposed by eminent Christians.

The possibility that Darwin might have been wrong did not occur to many, although modern-day Creationism has upheld the integrity of Genesis and exposed the frailty of Darwin's theories. Even so, the accepted orthodoxy within the Church is that some sort of evolution occurred, and Genesis is not literally true.

A typical position is set out in the report, *Doctrine in the Church of England*, published in 1938 by the Archbishop's Commission on Christian Doctrine. The report said, in words which would be acceptable to many in the Church to-day,

> 'It is to be recognised that the Christian doctrine of Creation ... leaves abundant room for a variety of theories as to the evolution of the world ... No objection to a theory of evolution can be drawn from the two Creation narratives in Gen.i. and ii., since it is generally agreed among educated Christians that these are mythological in origin, and that their value for us is symbolic rather than historical. It is to be noted that a non-literal interpretation of these chapters is to be found in some ancient Fathers.' [1]

Whilst the report was not intended to be an authoritative statement of the faith of the Church of England, the above passage shows how far the Laodicean spirit had permeated the Church. Evolution, which is definitely not what the Bible teaches, was assumed to be the truth, and the Bible had to be explained accordingly. Instead of being accepted as historical fact, Genesis 1 and 2 were turned into myth and symbol. This position was bolstered by appealing to education and to some unnamed ancient fathers of the Church. The world had invaded the Church, and was altering its foundation documents.

In modern times the Pope has added his weight to the concept of evolution by commenting that,

> 'new knowledge leads to recognition of the theory of evolution as more than a hypothesis.' [2]

It is therefore no real surprise to find a Polish Roman Catholic scientist commenting that in his country 'the

Catholic clergy, even the bishops, are the most ardent defenders of evolution.'[3]

Following the controversy over evolution and creation, and the almost complete capitulation by the Church, the destruction of the Bible continued with ever increasing velocity. The world tore the Scriptures to shreds and consigned them to the flames. At the same time many Christian leaders and scholars wrote hundreds of books, and preached thousands of sermons, which erased or altered inconvenient parts of the Bible.

This has led to a severe undermining of the authority of the Bible, and we have now reached the state where a leading Anglican bishop can openly describe the Bible as 'flawed and fallible.'[4]

A particularly chilling comment appears in the book, *Liberating the Gospels*, by the Rt Rev. John Spong, the then Bishop of New Jersey, in which he dismissed most of the Gospel narrative as unhistorical. He wrote of the birth stories of our Lord,

> 'A literal view of the Gospels becomes untenable. There might well have been no such person in history called Joseph, the spouse of Mary, the earthly father of Jesus, who was said to have guarded the manger when Jesus was born. Indeed, there was in all probability no manger. There were also no literal shepherds, no angels, no guiding star, no magi, and no flight into Egypt. There was not even a journey to Bethlehem by one who was "great with child".'[5]

The author then (correctly) claimed that his views were not unusual.

> 'To dismiss these parts of the biblical tradition as unhistorical legends is not particularly radical. That has been done hundreds of times before ... That has become almost tolerable, even among religious conservatives.'[6]

Another writer sums up the present situation as follows,

'While some still affirm it (i.e. the Bible) as the infallible and inerrant word of God, others treat it virtually as a secular book, feeling free to accept or reject whatever parts may or may not appeal to them. Between these two extremes lie those who accept in principle its inspiration and centrality for Christian doctrine, but recognize that it must be studied critically and in context, and that its teachings cannot simply be removed from their original settings and mechanically applied to very different circumstances.'[7]

In actual fact, there are but two positions: those who accept the Scripture as the infallible and inerrant Word of God, and those who do not.

II

The modification of the Scriptures has deeply affected the grass roots of the Church. The ubiquitous 'only Paul' syndrome is one example of this process.

Many of Paul's teachings directly contradict modern liberal assumptions. *'I permit no woman to teach or to have authority over men'* (1 Timothy 2.12) is irreconcilable with feminism, and *'Do not be deceived; neither the immoral, nor idolaters, nor adulterers, nor sexual perverts . . . will inherit the kingdom of God'* (1 Corinthians 6:9, 10), is at total variance with present-day concepts of sexual inclusiveness.

This antithesis creates a problem for those who accept modern standards and attitudes as the benchmark by which all shall be judged. Some, such as Michael Vasey in his book, *Strangers and Friends,*[8] attempt to reinterpret Paul's teaching from their own particular, in this case homosexual, standpoint. Others assume Paul is wrong, and try to remove the offending doctrines from the canon of Christian belief by declaring, 'That is only Paul', or 'That is just Paul's opinion.'[9]

The 'only Paul' syndrome is the end-product of many generations of critical destruction. The authenticity of Paul's letters has been challenged, with experts claiming that some were not written by the apostle. Also various theologians have tried to draw a distinction between the teachings of Jesus and those of Paul, claiming Paul changed and corrupted the original gospel. As one commentator succinctly puts it,

'According to this view, Paul was the arch-corrupter of the Gospel. God sent His Son to be a solution; Paul made Him a problem.'[10]

Although scholars disagree about which letters are genuine and exactly where Paul differs from Jesus, the underlying implication is that a considerable amount of Paul's teaching can be ignored. Therefore the way is clear to reject everything in Paul which contravenes the spirit of the age.

'Only Paulism' finds expression in both pulpit and liturgy. The formula, 'This is the word of the Lord', appointed to be said after the Epistle in the Anglican Communion service, is a particular stumbling block, and various verbal devices are used to overcome it.

The modern antipathy to some of Paul's teachings is well expressed at the popular level by Martin Palmer, in his book *Living Christianity*. The author is a lay theologian, religious adviser on ecology matters to HRH Prince Philip, and Director of the multifaith organisation, International Consultancy on Religion, Education and Culture. He holds that,

'There is no question that Paul does reflect or even over emphasise the contemporary view of his time that women should be subservient to their husbands and that the only role for women is in the home ... He certainly viewed sex as a necessary evil.'

'Paul also loaded the young faith with some pretty undesirable social teachings which owed more to his views and to the values of his culture than they did to the freedom brought by Jesus Christ.'[11]

Having removed all non-politically correct views from Paul's writings, the author then transforms the remainder of Paul's teaching into a multifaith liberal gospel. He claims that,

'Paul ... took the vision of Christianity as he found it and expanded it to take on board and absorb new world views.'

And he further claims,

'The Christianity which Paul so strongly fought for ... was in fact a pluralist faith. Paul helped Christianity spread by drawing upon Biblical and non-Biblical insights, terms of references and beliefs.'[12]

The consequences of the 'only Paul' syndrome are typical of all compromises. They include uncertainty about the authority of the Bible, and divisions concerning the teachings of the Christian faith.

It is germane to note that some exponents of 'only Paulism' are inconsistent. They do not accept Paul's teaching on homosexuality but are quick to claim a 'Pauline exception' in support of the remarriage of divorcees.[13]

III

Another example of our Laodicean attitude is the various inclusive translations of the Scriptures. Here the actual text of Scripture is changed. Words and phrases of the original Hebrew and Greek which do not conform to the dictates of modern political correctness are altered or suppressed.

Although contemporary views on sexual, racial and religious inclusiveness have instigated these translations, the dominant influence has been modern feminism. As one writer puts it,

> 'Modern feminists affirm the essential value of women as people, not just as wives and mothers. They oppose "exclusive" language (for example, the use of "man", "men" and the masculine pronoun to refer to women) and the assumption that the male is the norm of the species.' [14]

There are a whole range of inclusive translations, ranging from the moderate to the extreme. Two comparatively moderate versions are the inclusive New International Version, and the New Revised Standard Version.

This latter version is the work of an ecumenical team of translators from the Roman Catholic, Orthodox and Protestant churches. It is claimed in the preface that,

> 'During the almost half a century since the publication of the RSV, many in the churches have become sensitive to the danger of linguistic sexism arising from the inherent bias of the English language towards the masculine gender, a bias that in the case of the Bible has often restricted or obscured the meaning of the original text.' [15]

The translators had a mandate that 'in references to men and women, masculine-oriented language should be eliminated as far as this can be done without altering passages that reflect the historical situation of ancient patriarchal culture'.[16] They claimed that 'in the vast majority of cases ... inclusiveness has been attained by simple rephrasing or by introducing plural forms when this does not distort the meaning of the passage.' [17]

A publicity leaflet fleshes out the strategy.

> 'The NRSV uses "inclusive language"; that is, it uses words such as "children" rather than the male-biased

"son" and "ancestors" rather than "fathers", where the original languages clearly include both sexes.'[18]

Examples abound. *'Man shall not live by bread alone'* (Matthew 4:4) becomes *'One does not live by bread alone'*. Jesus' words to Simon and Andrew, *'I will make you become fishers of men'* (Mark 1:17) is changed to *'I will make you fish for people'*. Yet the original Greek in both texts uses 'man' and 'men' respectively.

The term 'brethren' in Romans 10:1 and many other places, becomes 'brothers and sisters'. Similarly, the statement in 1 John 4:21 that, *'he who loves God should love his brother also'* has been changed to *'those who love God must love their brothers and sisters also'*.

The word *'son'* has received the same treatment. Revelation 21:7 reads,

> *'He who conquers shall have this heritage, and I will be his God and he shall be my son.'*

This appears as,

> *'Those who conquer will inherit these things, and I will be their God and they will be my children.'*

The original Greek text of this verse uses the masculine 'he' and 'son', and is in the singular.

However masculine nouns and pronouns are used for all three Persons of the Holy Trinity. God is still the Father and Jesus remains the Son of God.

It could be argued that many of these changes make no practical or theological difference. This is a moot point, but what cannot be accepted is the principle on which these changes are based. The Word of God is being deliberately altered to suit the dictates of modern thought, and once that process starts there is no telling where it will end. It is obvious that, to the translators, fidelity to the Word of God is not as important as following the spirit of the age. It is, as one speaker has remarked,

> '... another great concession of principle, which could only happen in an age of spiritual and theological weakness.'[19]

Not all Christians approve of inclusive language translations. The Pope has forbidden his flock to use the New Revised Standard Version as it is not a faithful translation.[20] Nevertheless inclusive language Bibles have been accepted in Britain. They are published by reputable firms and are readily available in Christian and secular bookshops.

Adjustment of the Scriptures in any way is the father and mother of all compromise. As we look at other Laodicean accommodations which are rampant in the Church we will see that underneath all is a reshaping of scriptural teaching.

References

1. *Doctrine in the Church of England*, SPCK, 1938, p. 45.
2. 'Creation', *The Journal of the Creation Science Movement*, Vol. 10 No. 1, March 1997, p. 10.
3. M. Giertych, 'Plant Geneticist says No to Evolution!' *Pamphlet 311*, Creation Science Movement, March 1997, p. 4.
4. Richard F. Holloway, 'Getting Connected', The Lesbian and Gay Christians 22nd Annual Lecture, St. Alban's, London 18.4.1998.
5. J.S. Spong, *Liberating the Gospels*, Harper San Francisco, 1996, p. 322.
6. *ibid*. p. 322.
7. Ruth B. Edwards, *The Case for Women's Ministry*, SPCK, 1989, p. 3.
8. Michael Vasey, *Strangers and Friends*, Hodder and Stoughton, 1995.
9. In 1932, the well-known Bible expositor, C.H. Dodd wrote in the Introduction to his commentary on Romans that 'in the main what he (Paul) says seems to me to be profoundly true,' but he also said that, 'sometimes I think Paul is wrong, and I have ventured to say so.' *Epistle to the Romans*, Hodder and Stoughton,1932, p. xxxv.
10. James S. Stewart, *A Man in Christ*, Hodder and Stoughton, 1946, p. 18. Reproduced by permission of Hodder and Stoughton Ltd.
11. Martin Palmer, *Living Christianity*, Element Books, 1993, pp. 22, 23.
12. *ibid*. p. 22.
13. See chapter 12, pp. 91, 92.
14. Ruth B. Edwards, *The Case for Women's Ministry*, p. 121.

15. Bruce M. Metzger, 'To the Reader', *New Revised Standard Version*, Collins, 1989.
16. *ibid.*
17. *ibid.*
18. NRSV a standard for our times. A publicity leaflet by Cambridge University Press.
19. Roger Beckwith, 'Inclusive Language', An address at the Prayer Book Society AGM, 22.6.1996, 'Faith and Worship', The Prayer Book Society, Advent 1996, p. 15.
20. *ibid.* p. 15.

INTERFAITH COMPROMISE

Chapter 9

The Only True God

'Turn to me and be saved, all the ends of the earth!
For I am God, and there is no other.'
(Isaiah 45:22)

I

Over a hundred years ago, in 1893, a groundbreaking inter-faith conference, known as the World Parliament of Religions, was held in Chicago. Its aim was to show the contribution made to humanity by religion.

Although the conference attracted over 150,000 people from many different faiths, not everyone approved. The Archbishop of Canterbury, Dr E.W. Benson, had been invited, but refused to go on the grounds that the Parliament implied that all religions were equal and so compromised the uniqueness of Jesus Christ.

Today Dr Benson's attitude would strike many people as old-fashioned and judgemental. In our liberal western civilis-ation an increasing number of people believe that all religions lead to God.

There are many reasons for this inclusive position. So far as Great Britain is concerned, one important factor was the rise of the British Empire. As the Empire expanded during the 19th century many people left these islands for far-flung corners of the globe. There they made contact with other religions and were fascinated by what they discovered. In later years modern communications and the mass tourist industry have had similar effects.

Large-scale immigration has also made us more aware of non-Christian religions. Although some immigrants are Christian, others are Muslim, Hindu or Buddhist, and it is now commonplace to see mosques and Hindu temples in our towns and cities.

Immigration has led to a genuine and healthy desire for racial harmony. In order to promote good race relations, many have wrongly equated religion with race. They have held, broadly speaking, that Christianity is associated with white nations, Islam with Arabian and black civilisations, and Hinduism and Buddhism with Asian culture. Thus, for the sake of racial integration, we are encouraged to believe that all faiths are equal.

The emergence of the New Age Movement has accelerated the idea that all religions have a common basis and goal. New Age is a very diffuse phenomenon, which gathers within itself a whole range of spiritual experience.

'The attitude adopted towards the world and people is holistic ... It is inevitable that the holistic approach, with its sense of one self, one world, and one universe, should also press the idea of one religion.'[1]

This means that New Age followers see truth in all religions, and extract what they find helpful from each. The one thing New Age devotees hate is the fundamentalist claim that one faith is right and the others wrong.

II

What, then, was behind Dr Benson's thinking when he refused to go to Chicago in 1893? To put it simply, it was the teaching of the Bible, which states that there is one God, and the only way to know Him is through Jesus Christ.

The ten commandments, which were given to the Israelites after they had fled from Egypt, teach that God alone must be worshipped. The first commandment states,

> *'You shall have no other gods before me.'* (Exodus 20:3)

and the second,

> *'You shall not make for yourself a graven image, or any likeness of anything that is in heaven above, or that is in the earth beneath, or that is in the water under the earth; you shall not bow down to them or serve them; for I the LORD your God am a jealous God...'* (Exodus 20:4, 5)

Forty years later, immediately before the Jews entered into their inheritance, God reiterated these laws, and applied them in detail to the situation the Israelites would soon face. In particular, they had to destroy everything connected with the pagan gods previously worshipped in the land.

> *'You shall surely destroy all the places where the nations whom you shall dispossess served their gods, upon the high mountains and upon the hills and under every green tree; you shall tear down their altars, and dash in pieces their pillars, and burn their Asherim with fire; you shall hew down the graven images of their gods, and destroy their name out of that place.'* (Deuteronomy 12:2, 3)

The false gods had to be completely forgotten.

> *'After they have been destroyed before you, ... do not inquire about their gods, saying, "How did these nations serve their gods? – that I may also do likewise".'*
> (Deuteronomy 12:30)

In both Old and New Testaments there is the glorious refrain, that God is one, and He alone should be worshipped and adored. Isaiah, chapter 45, is an example of this. Speaking through Isaiah, God says,

> *'I am the LORD, and there is no other, besides me there is no God.'* (Isaiah 45:5)

He is God, not only of the Jews, but of all the peoples of the earth, and He longs for the day when,

> *'... men may know, from the rising of the sun and from the west, that there is none besides me.'* (Isaiah 45:6)

At present many people worship idols, *'that cannot save'* (Isaiah 45:20), but one day, God promises,

> *'To me every knee shall bow, every tongue shall swear.'*
> (Isaiah 45:23)

Then all other religions and gods will be no more. People from one end of the earth to the other will worship the one true God.

The Jews of old had great problems with this commandment, for they lived in a world of many faiths. Egypt, where they had once lived, had a whole gallery of gods, as had the great civilisations to the East, such as Assyria and Babylonia. It would, therefore, have been much easier to go along with the world and worship many deities.

The whole Jewish history up to the exile in Babylon and beyond is a story of how the people kept turning to other gods. Although God sent great prophets such as Elijah and Jeremiah to bring the people back to Him, and even though brave and courageous kings such as Hezekiah and Josiah tried to purge the land of idols, yet time and again, the Jews went back to these false gods.

> *'They mingled with the nations and learned to do as they did. They served their idols, which became a snare to them.'*
> (Psalm 106:35, 36)

III

The Jews of Jesus' day had learned the lessons of the past, and they clung fiercely to the belief that there is only one God, who alone should be worshipped.

Our Lord Himself underlined this truth. He quoted Deuteronomy 6:4,

> *'Hear, O Israel: The Lord our God is one Lord; and you shall love the Lord your God with all your heart, and with all your soul, and with all your might.'*

'This', He said, *'is the great and first commandment'* (Matthew 22:38).

Yet Jesus went further. He claimed that there was only one way to know God, and that was through Him. When talking to His apostles on the evening of His arrest, He said,

> *'I am the way, and the truth, and the life; no one comes to the Father, but by me.'* (John 14:6)

This exclusive faith was proclaimed by the early Church to both Jew and Gentile. When Peter and John were dragged before the Jewish Council to explain the healing of a cripple, Peter said of Jesus,

> *'This is the stone which was rejected by you builders, but which has become the head of the corner. And there is salvation in no one else, for there is no other name under heaven given among men by which we must be saved.'*
> (Acts 4:11, 12)

The Gentiles, who worshipped many gods, received the same message. When Paul and Silas were in prison in Philippi there was a great earthquake, which resulted in the prison doors being opened and the prisoner's chains loosed. The

distraught jailer was about to commit suicide, but Paul
reassured him that no one had escaped. This led the jailer
to ask,

> *'Men, what must I do to be saved?'*   (Acts 16:30)

Paul replied,

> *'Believe in the Lord Jesus, and you will be saved, you and
> your household.'*   (Acts 16:31)

There was no question of Paul urging him to be faithful to
the Greek gods which were worshipped in Philippi. The jailer
had to make a radical break with his pagan past and turn to
Christ.

As Paul said in his letter to Timothy,

> *'There is one God, and there is one mediator between God
> and men, the man Christ Jesus, who gave Himself as a
> ransom for all.'*   (1 Timothy 2:5, 6)

The complaint of Demetrius, the silversmith of Ephesus,
that

> *'Paul has persuaded and turned away a considerable
> company of people, saying that gods made with hands are
> not gods'*   (Acts 19:26)

shows how clearly the gospel had been heard and understood, even by those who refused to accept it.

IV

The post-apostolic Church held the same faith. Christian
evangelists urged people to turn away from other religions
and believe in Christ. This spelt trouble for Christians in the

Roman Empire. Because they rejected the old gods, and refused to take part in emperor worship, they were accused of atheism and treason. Both were punishable offences, and many Christians were martyred on this account.

One such was the philosopher Justin. He and his Christian friends were arrested in Rome in the year 165, and brought before a prefect named Rusticus. Having established that all the arrested were Christians, Rusticus urged them to worship the pagan gods.

'Agree together', he said, 'and sacrifice with one accord to the gods.'

Justin replied, 'No one who is rightly minded turns from true belief to false.'

Rusticus then warned them, 'If you do not obey, you shall be punished without mercy.'

To this Justin replied,

'If we are punished for the sake of our Lord Jesus Christ we hope to be saved, for this shall be our salvation and confidence before the more terrible judgement-seat of our Lord and Saviour which shall judge the whole world.'

The other accused Christian said,

'Do what you will. For we are Christians and offer no sacrifice to idols.'

At this the prisoners, glorifying God, were led out, whipped and beheaded.[2]

There was clearly no multifaith compromise for Justin and his friends. Other religions were seen as false beliefs. Only faith in Jesus brought salvation.

As St. Augustine of Hippo said,

'All truth is of Him who says, "I am the truth".'[3]

V

A brief comparison of Christianity with other world religions shows the logical impossibility of holding the oneness of all faiths.

Islam does not believe that Jesus was the Son of God. According to the Koran, the angel Gabriel appeared to Mohammed, and said that God could not have a son. Hence,

> 'Jesus, son of Mary, is only an apostle of God . . . Far be it from His glory that He should have a son.' [4]

Yet the Bible says that the angel Gabriel appeared to Mary and told her,

> ' . . . *the child to be born will be called holy, the Son of God.'*
> (Luke 1:35)

Here is a basic conflict between Islam and Christianity. Jesus is either the Son of God, or He is not. Both beliefs cannot be true.

Another incompatibility is that Islam not only denies Jesus' resurrection, but holds that He did not die on the cross. The Koran says,

> 'They slew him not, and they crucified him not, but they only had his likeness.' [5]

Most followers of Islam believe that Judas, not Jesus, was crucified. Therefore, they argue, when Jesus' followers saw Him after the crucifixion they wrongly thought He had risen from the dead.

Yet the Bible teaches the direct opposite. Paul, for example, states that it is *'of first importance'*,

> '*that Christ died for our sins in accordance with the Scriptures, that He was buried, that He was raised on the third day in accordance with the Scriptures.'*   (1 Corinthians 15:3, 4)

We see similar disparities if we compare Christianity with Hinduism. A basic belief of Hinduism is reincarnation. According to this doctrine, 'every being at death passes from one existence to another as determined by the karma, the sum of the good and evil deeds in the existence just completed. A new existence awaits each dying being; whether it be as divinity, person, animal or inmate of hell is decided by the person's merit.'[6]

The Christian faith rejects all thought of reincarnation. We have but one life on earth.

> *'It is appointed for men to die once, and after that comes judgement.'*   (Hebrews 9:27)

Both Hinduism and Christianity speak of salvation, but they mean very different things. For the Hindu salvation consists of escaping the endless cycle of death and reincarnation, and is achieved by either philosophical knowledge, worship, works or meditation. These ways of salvation are known as yogas, a term which is well known in our civilisation.

The Christian holds that salvation is from sin. We are all sinners, and unless our sins are forgiven we cannot reach God and be with Him eternally. Forgiveness comes to us through the sacrifice of Jesus on the cross.

> *'He Himself bore our sins in His body on the tree, that we might die to sin and live to righteousness.'*   (1 Peter 2:24)

We cannot earn our salvation through knowledge, worship, works or meditation. We are saved through faith in Jesus, and no other way.

> *'For by grace you have been saved through faith; and this is not your own doing, it is the gift of God.'*   (Ephesians 2:8)

Thus Hinduism and Christianity hold opposing beliefs on the central issues of life. Both cannot be right, for one set of beliefs automatically excludes the other.

In a similar way Buddhism, in all its diverse forms, has beliefs which are diametrically opposed to the Christian faith. The Buddhist faith says nothing about the existence of a personal God, or even of a God at all. As one Buddhist writer put it,

> 'The Buddhist teaching on God, in the sense of an ultimate Reality, is neither agnostic ... nor vague, but clear and logical. Whatever Reality may be, it is beyond the conception of the finite intellect; it follows that attempts at description are misleading, unprofitable, a waste of time. For these good reasons the Buddha maintained about Reality "a noble silence".'[7]

For the Buddhist, 'there is no God in the Christian sense.'[8] Christianity, on the other hand, gloriously affirms that there is a personal God, who knows and loves us, and has revealed Himself, so that we may know and love Him.

It is therefore obvious that Christians and Buddhists cannot worship together.

> 'Worship ... is an acknowledgement of that which one reveres; primarily it is absolute reverence for absolute or divine worth ... For the Buddhist, there is no supernal worth to be worshipped in the sense of adoration.'[9]

Further, Buddhism has no concept of sin or conscience. The Christian, however, believes that,

> *'Your iniquities have made a separation between you and your God, and your sins have hid His face from you so that He does not hear.'*   (Isaiah 59:2)

Even Judaism, the soil in which Christianity has its roots, has irreconcilable differences with the Christian faith, for it rejects the Messiahship of Jesus. Although the life and work of Jesus are foretold in a remarkable way in the Old Testament, many Jews of Jesus' day did not see this. As Paul said,

'Whenever Moses is read a veil lies over their minds.'
(2 Corinthians 3:15)

Yet Paul could rejoice as he testified from personal experience,

'When a man turns to the Lord the veil is removed.'
(2 Corinthians 3:16)

Thus, for the Christian believer, there can be no truck or compromise with any other religion. If we wish all men to be saved, then we have to point to Jesus and show that He alone is the way to God.

References

1. Wesley Carr, *Manifold Wisdom*, SPCK, 1991, pp. 16, 46.
2. *A New Eusebius*, ed. J. Stevenson, SPCK, 1968, p. 30.
3. Augustine of Hippo, *On Christian Doctrine*, trans. J.F. Shaw, *A Select Library of the Nicene and Post-Nicene Fathers of the Christian Church*, ed. Philip Schaff, The Christian Literature Co., Buffalo, 1887, p. 521.
4. *The Koran*, trans. J.M. Rodwell, Everyman Edition, 1909, Surah 4.169.
5. *ibid*. Surah 4.157.
6. L. Aletrino, *Six World Religions*, trans. M. Furan, SCM, 1967, p. 42.
7. C. Humphreys, *Buddhism*, Penguin Books, 1951, p. 79, © Christmas Humphreys, 1951. Reproduced by permission of Penguin Books Ltd.
8. Winston L. King, *Buddhism and Christianity*, George Allen and Unwin Ltd, 1963, p. 19.
9. *ibid*. p. 24.

Chapter 10

The Denial of the Lord

'Therefore God has highly exalted Him
and bestowed on Him the name which is above every name,
that at the name of Jesus every knee should bow.'
(Philippians 2:9, 10)

I

In 1996 a leading churchman wrote, with approval, that

'The coming together of world religions, however tentative and hesitant, is the most significant religious fact in our contemporary world society.' [1]

The reaction of three Archbishops of Canterbury to the World Congress of Faiths illustrates how this coming together has led to the abandonment of our belief in Jesus as the only way to God.

The Congress was founded in the 1930s by Sir Francis Younghusband, a soldier and explorer, who said that through his travels he had discovered a new depth to the Christian faith, and found great profundity and beauty in other religions. In 1903 he had a spiritual experience in Tibet which led him to believe in the mystical unity of all mankind and all religions. Throughout the rest of his life he worked that people might share his vision, without abandoning their own particular faith.

Although Sir Francis considered himself a Christian, his beliefs were far from orthodox. He appeared to believe that Jesus was but a good man, whose life was an example for posterity. He claimed that,

> 'joy ... was at the heart of Christ's message. Hindu, Buddhist and Muslim saints had declared the same, and the Psalms were full of its expression.'[2]

At its inception the World Congress of Faiths reflected Younghusband's ideals. Its objectives were, 'to promote a spirit of fellowship among mankind through religion', and 'to awaken and develop world loyalty, while allowing complete freedom for diversities of men, nations and faiths.'[3]

This meant that,

> 'The position of the Congress ruled out the view that any one religion had a monopoly of truth, assuming that, despite differences, the world religions have an affinity and share a recognition of spiritual reality and ethical values.'[4]

This is not, of course, what the Bible teaches.

The first meeting of the Congress was held in London in 1936, and the Archbishop of Canterbury, C.G. Lang, was asked to preside. He refused, and in a letter to Commander Campbell at Buckingham Palace, the Archbishop said he did not accept the invitation because,

> 'this might be taken to imply that I thought Christianity was only one of many religions in spite of being as I believed the true religion based upon Divine revelation.'[5]

Lang also advised the King to decline an invitation to preside at the opening session, but admitted that 'some respectable Church of England clergy had given the Congress their sanction.'[6]

In 1969 Archbishop Michael Ramsay declined an invitation to address the Congress for similar reasons. He gave two particular objections. The first was that he did not believe ' "religion" ... contained the essence of what is good ... Not all "religion" is good, and some of the religion, under the Hindu banner "seems to be very bad indeed".'[7] His other objection was that the 'World Congress of Faiths ideology is being used by non-Christians in order to propagate their own belief in a diffused view of deity and revelation at the expense of the distinctive Christian belief in particularity.'[8]

But in 1986 Archbishop Robert Runcie accepted an invitation from the World Congress to speak at the annual Sir Francis Younghusband Memorial Lecture.

The very acceptance of this invitation, as well as the content of the lecture, showed a huge departure from the position of Archbishops Lang and Ramsay.

Dr Runcie commenced his lecture by saying,

> 'What a pleasure and privilege it is for me to give the Sir Francis Younghusband Memorial Lecture during this 50th anniversary year of the World Congress of Faiths.'[9]

He then claimed that faiths other than Christianity 'are genuine mansions of the Spirit with many rooms to be discovered,'[10] and quoted, with approval, some words of Sir Francis Younghusband,

> 'All the centuries that the Spirit of God had been working in Christians, He must also have been working in Hindus, Buddhists, Muslims and others.'[11]

Hence 'we must learn to recognize the work of the Spirit at the centre of each of our faiths',[12] and 'from the perspective of faith, different world religions can be seen as different gifts of the Spirit to humanity.'[13]

During the course of his lecture, the Archbishop actually denied the finality and completeness of the Christian faith. He said,

'It takes humility and sincerity to concede that there is a certain incompleteness in each of our traditions ... We must also recognize that ultimately all religions possess a provisional, interim character as ways and signs to help us in our pilgrimage to Ultimate Truth and Perfection.'[14]

Thus it was that Christian truth was sacrificed to the spirit of an age which, according to Dr Runcie, is characterised by

'a search for some "golden core" of religion independent of any specific tradition.'[15]

II

The growth of interfaith worship is another example of our compromise with the world. Although interfaith services have taken place at various venues for decades, the matter came into public prominence in the 1980s, due to a number of high-profile acts of worship.

Two services were held at Assisi, in the Upper Basilica of St. Francis, in 1986. The first, described as an 'interfaith ceremony',[16] was held in September to celebrate the 25th Anniversary of the World Wide Fund for Nature, and involved representatives from Christianity, Buddhism, Islam, Judaism and Hinduism. The service started with a muezzin calling in Arabic from the bell tower, as from a minaret, and included rituals drawn from each faith. Although the Minister General of the Franciscan order told the congregation that 'No one pretends that our respective beliefs are or can be held in common', yet he gave the invitation, 'Let us now, each according to the wealth of our own religious traditions, celebrate our common concern for the future of the world.'[17] An Italian journalist wrote,

> 'Giotto's frescoes of the life of St. Francis had to wait more than 500 years to witness Buddhist, Hindu, Islamic and Jewish rituals within the nave of the church where the Roman Catholic patron saint of ecology lies buried. Nothing remotely like this has happened before.'[18]

The second service, held a month later, was instigated by the Pope, who invited 'leaders of Christian Churches, and other world religions'[19] to meet at Assisi to pray for peace. About sixty Christian representatives were present, and around forty from other faiths. The Pope welcomed the participants in the church of Santa Maria degli Angeli, and then each religious group met separately to pray according to its own tradition. In the evening the whole gathering assembled in the Upper Basilica of St. Francis, where representatives of each faith offered prayers in the presence of all. This was followed by 'a common act expressing the will for peace of all present.' The Pope then addressed the assembly, and the day closed with a sign of peace.[20]

It was strongly denied that this was interfaith worship, but the fact that the Pope summoned representatives of the world's religions for prayer gave these faiths a validity which is denied to them by Scripture. The Christian faith teaches that prayer must be offered through Jesus. Laodicean compromise had reached the very top of the Roman Catholic Church.

It is, of course, right to care for the world and to pray for peace. But it is not right to deny the uniqueness of Jesus, who alone will bring about a new earth and everlasting peace. Neither is it right to use a Christian church for prayers to gods which are no gods. It is salutary to note that in 1997 the Upper Basilica, including the bell tower, was severely damaged by an earthquake.

A well publicised interfaith gathering in England was the 1989 Canterbury Festival of Faith and the Environment. This weekend festival was promoted by the World Wide Fund for Nature, and organised on their behalf by the inter-faith organisation, International Consultancy on Religions, Education and Culture.

The Festival started with three pilgrimages, led respectively by a Christian, a Bahai and a Hindu. On arrival in Canterbury, on Friday, September 15th, the groups prayed together in the cathedral, using a liturgy which contained no reference to Jesus.

The next day members of different faiths held worship and celebrations on Christian property throughout the city. In the evening the cathedral hosted a Celebration, described as a celebration of 'the Forest', (with a capital F), which drew 'upon the teaching and beliefs of many faiths.'[21] During the celebration a choir sang in worship to the trees, using the words, 'We worship them'. The celebration also included teaching on Buddhism.

Extracts from Bahai, Hindu, Muslim, Sikh and Buddhist writings were printed for the cathedral Sunday morning Eucharist, and offered to the worshippers as resources for reflection.[22]

The Canterbury event was neither the first nor the last interfaith meeting in an English cathedral. Newcastle, Winchester, Coventry, Leicester and Bristol cathedrals have hosted such gatherings, and Westminster Abbey has for many years held a multifaith Commonwealth Day service. Space does not allow us to go into the details of such services, but one example shows their flavour. At a Creation Harvest Liturgy in Winchester Cathedral in 1987, writings from the Bahai, Buddhist, Hindu, Islamic, Taoist, Jewish and Sikh faiths were offered as 'sources of prayer, inspiration and reflection.'[23] Members of other faiths were present, and although they did not participate in the Communion, they joined with the Christians at the end of the service in launching the Rainbow Covenant, 'which is designed for all people of goodwill.'[24] This involved members of the congre-gation tying rainbow threads round one another's wrists, as a sign of their commitment to world conservation. Such a ceremony is full of Hindu and New Age overtones. In Hinduism 'these multi-coloured strings are a means of channelling psychic rays',[25] and the rainbow is the adopted symbol of the New Age movement.

In 1992 the Church of England General Synod Board of Mission published a report entitled *Multi-Faith Worship?* This was issued as a result of the growing number of interfaith services in England, including those in Anglican cathedrals.

The general tenor of the report is Laodicean in that it goes along with the inclusive attitudes of the age, and is, on balance, in favour of interfaith worship. Although it says 'no-one intends to deny Christ or act contrary to Christian doctrine',[26] yet it attempts to show that the Bible supports interfaith worship.

Using two passages from the book of Daniel the report suggests that Kings Nebuchadnezzar and Darius worshipped the Lord under the name of a different god (Daniel 4:34–37; 6:25–27). It also uses Malachi 1:11 to draw similar conclusions about worship by the Gentile nations in general. This verse says,

> *'"For from the rising of the sun to its setting my name is great among the nations, and in every place incense is offered to my name, and a pure offering; for my name is great among the nations," says the* LORD *of hosts.'*

The report comments that this verse suggests 'that the names of the gods addressed' by people of other nations 'are in some sense identical with that of Yahweh, the LORD of hosts.'[27]

In fact none of these passages, nor any other in the Bible, support interfaith worship. The passages in Daniel show that both kings were explicitly worshipping the Lord. The passage in Malachi is not easy to understand and has received many interpretations. Its basic message is that the Gentiles, or Gentile believers in the Lord, are honouring Him more than the Jewish priests in Jerusalem. The one thing it does not mean is that the pagan gods worshipped by the Gentiles are in any way the same as the Lord. It is the consistent witness of Scripture that the gods of the nations are only *'gods of wood and stone, the work of men's hands, that neither see, nor hear, nor eat, nor smell'* (Deuteronomy 4:28).

It is, of course, obvious that once it is said that the gods of other nations are in some way identical to the Lord, it is easy to go a step further and say that the worship offered by Muslims, Hindus and Buddhists today is really worship of the one true God.

The report also gives suggestions for 'Multi-faith services with an agreed common order',[28] in which it proposes that 'items should be selected to emphasise what all present hold in common, but without glossing over differences or giving the impression that none exist.'[29] It is also suggested that readings in multifaith services may be from 'the classical scriptures'.[30] The Word of God is thereby put alongside the sacred writings of other religions with the implication that they are all of equal value.

References

1. Rev. Dr Edward Carpenter, in the Foreword to *A Wider Vision*, © Marcus Braybrooke, 1996. Reproduced by permission of Oneworld Publications.
2. M. Braybrooke, *op. cit.* p. 31.
3. *ibid.* p. 93.
4. *ibid.* p. 47.
5. *ibid.* p. 36.
6. *ibid.* p. 36.
7. *ibid.* p. 83.
8. *ibid.* p. 83.
9. R. Runcie, 'Christianity and World Religions', World Congress of Faiths, 1986, p. 3.
10. *ibid.* p. 3.
11. *ibid.* p. 4.
12. *ibid.* p. 9.
13. *ibid.* p. 11.
14. *ibid.* p. 10.
15. *ibid.* p. 3.
16. 'The New Road', *The Bulletin of the WWF Network on Conservation and Religion*, Issue No. 1, Winter 1986/87, p. 1.
17. *ibid.* p. 3.

18. *ibid.* p. 3.
19. *Church Times* 17.10.1986.
20. *ibid.*
21. Canterbury Festival of Faith and the Environment, WWF publicity leaflet.
22. T. Higton, 'The Canterbury Crime', *Christian Herald*, 30.9.1989.
23. Creation Harvest Liturgy, Winchester Cathedral, 4.10.1987, WWF, p. 21.
24. *ibid.* p. 1.
25. W. Carr, *Manifold Wisdom*, p. 140.
26. 'Multi-Faith Worship?', *General Synod Board of Mission*, Church House Publishing, 1992, p. 5. Extracts from 'Multi-Faith Worship?' are copyright © The Central Board of Finance of the Church of England, 1992; The Archbishops' Council, 1999 and are reproduced by permission.
27. *ibid.* p. 26.
28. *ibid.* pp. 51–56.
29. *ibid.* p. 53.
30. *ibid.* p. 55.

Chapter 11

Unfaithfulness Abounding

'For whoever is ashamed of me and of my words
in this adulterous and sinful generation,
of him will the Son of man also be ashamed,
when He comes in the glory of His Father
with the holy angels.'
(Mark 8:38)

I

The vexed question of the use of church buildings by adherents of other faiths is another facet of our growing interfaith compromise.

In 1983 the Church of England General Synod debated the motion that

> 'church buildings which have been declared redundant may in appropriate circumstances be made available to those of non-Christian faiths for the purpose of their worship'.[1]

The background to this debate was the proposed sale to the Sikhs of a church in Southampton. The bishops and the clergy accepted the motion, but it was defeated by the laity. Nevertheless the church was sold to the Sikhs.

In 1994 the Chancellor of York Minster suggested that 'the naves of many of our great cathedrals could become ... a space where all peoples of whatever culture or religion could feel themselves welcome and at home, a place where the existence and presence of the transcendent Creator God was acknowledged and promoted ... This would mean that the nave would be the natural and uncontested location for interfaith events, and for other religious bodies to hold their worship at the invitation of the dean and chapter.'[2] The choir of the cathedral would then be the place 'where the explicit Christian gospel is proclaimed'.[3]

1996 saw a report entitled *Communities and Buildings: Church of England premises and other faiths*, published by the Board of Mission of the General Synod of the Church of England. It considered the problems of selling or leasing Church of England churches and halls to those of other faiths, as well as the possibility of sharing buildings with them.

At the time the report was being prepared, the church in Southampton was the only consecrated church which had been sold to another faith. However, the Church of England had leased or sold some dedicated (as opposed to consecrated) church buildings, 'as well as a number of church halls, vicarages and other church property' to other faith groups.[4] In addition some Anglican churches had 'made their buildings available for use by Hindus, Muslims and Sikhs who do not have adequate premises of their own.'[5] On top of that 'there are many examples of Methodist, URC and other redundant churches becoming temples, gurdwaras or mosques.'[6]

Perhaps inevitably the report came to the conclusion,

'we believe that there are circumstances in which the use of church property can be offered with integrity to communities of other faiths, as part of a wider local community.'[7]

This conclusion seemed to spring from social, rather than doctrinal, concerns.

'In some English inner cities the sale of an unwanted church building to those of another faith community could be a powerful statement of Christian opposition to racism and xenophobia, and church commitment to the disadvantaged.'[8]

Although the report said that 'the Church must not enable attacks on its own Gospel',[9] it failed to recognise that allowing members of other faiths to use church buildings in itself constituted an attack upon the good news that Jesus is the only way to God.

After a debate in July 1996 the Synod took note of the report as providing 'the proper framework for policy-making about the use of church buildings by people of other faiths'.[10] By effectively accepting the report, the Synod has led the Church of England further away from the truth as it is in Christ.

II

Our Lord's great commission to go into the world, and *'make disciples of all nations'* (Matthew 28:18–20) inspired many Christians of the 19th century to go into unknown parts and seek converts for Christ. These incredibly brave and dedicated Christians had no doubt about the uniqueness of Jesus Christ.

This missionary work has continued into the 20th century, and is still operative today. Yet many in the Church have turned their back on it, and have even debunked the whole enterprise. Missionaries have been portrayed as representatives of Western culture, rather than ambassadors of Christ. Their work has been considered imperialist and racist. There is indeed some truth in these accusations, as none of the work we do for our Lord is ever perfect. Yet we have thrown out the baby with the bath water, and many Christians today feel a sense of embarrassment and guilt about missionary work.

Things have now gone further, and voices in the Church are saying that there is no need to reach out to people of other faiths. In his Sir Francis Younghusband Lecture of 1986, Dr Runcie told the story of a lady missionary in India. He put it as follows,

> 'I am reminded of a story told by Ninian Smart of the lady missionary who was driving him to hospital not far from Benares. They passed a shrine, and she remarked: "I'm always very sad to see the piety with which those Hindus worship at that shrine." He asked why. "Well" she said with a sort of simple finality, "there's no one there to hear them."' [11]

The Archbishop then commented,

> 'That "simple finality" has no place today.' [12]

In one stroke the New Testament gospel was demolished, and the ground cut from under all those who left home and security to bring the good news of Jesus to the farthest parts of the globe.

In a television interview in 1991 the Bishop of Oxford said,

> 'I don't think myself that Christians today should be targeting the Jews for conversion.' [13]

When asked if Jesus is the Messiah of the Jews, the bishop replied,

> 'I personally take the view that Christians need to adopt a new approach to Judaism and that we don't want to keep telling the Jews that Jesus is the Messiah.' [14]

It is not hard to imagine how St. Paul, who spent a considerable time telling his fellow Jews that Jesus was their

Messiah, would have reacted to these statements. Paul's message was always that the gospel

> *'is the power of God for salvation to every one who has faith, to the Jew first and also to the Greek.'* (Romans 1:16)

In 1992 the Archbishop of Canterbury, Dr Carey, refused to become patron of the Church's Ministry among the Jews, although many previous Archbishops had accepted this position. One aim of this Anglican Society is,

> 'Evangelism: To be workers with God in His continuing purpose for the Jewish people, both in Israel and world-wide, especially in seeking to lead them to faith in Jesus the Messiah as their only Saviour.' [15]

However, Dr Carey did agree to be president of the Council of Christians and Jews, an interfaith body antagonistic towards the conversion of Jews.

III

When the Decade of Evangelism was announced at the start of the 1990s, those of non-Christian faiths became worried that they would be targets for conversion. On expressing these concerns, they were assured by church leaders that this would not be the case.

Words spoken by the Archbishop of Canterbury in 1992 encapsulate this attempt to reassure. Speaking about the Decade, the Archbishop said,

> 'In relation to other faiths ... we should respect their integrity while proclaiming and acting out our own firm belief in Jesus Christ as our Lord. Deliberate confrontation with other faiths would be counterproductive and divisive. A predominantly Christian society nurtures tolerance and constructive relationships with minority

faiths: and the Christian Churches need to work with people of other faiths in combating the shallow materialism of much contemporary life. We must never hide our beliefs; nor would other faiths respect us if we did. But our mission is to society as a whole, to all who have ears to hear, and especially to those who are half-hearted in their Christian commitment or have lost their faith altogether. Friction with minority faiths is an unproductive distraction from the enormous, positive agenda of the Decade.' [16]

That evangelism should be mainly restricted to lukewarm and lapsed Christians is a new position for Christians, and to undergird it the meaning of two key words, 'evangelism' and 'proselytism', have been changed.

In normal English a proselyte is someone who has converted from one faith to another. This meaning is found in the New Testament. [17] Within our multifaith context it has now become fashionable to give the word 'proselytism' a bad connotation. Hence,

'Proselytism is the imposition of my faith on you, not taking into account your culture, your needs and your history.' [18]

This is then contrasted with 'evangelism', which instead of preaching the gospel to the unconverted becomes, 'the genuine love for another person which takes on board your culture, your present understanding and allows you room to grow.' [19]

Thus the idea is given, almost subconsciously, that it is not good to seek to win people from other faiths.

A similar misuse of words is seen in the meaning given to the term 'ecumenical.' Originally this meant the promotion of unity between the Christian churches throughout the world. Now it is used to mean the coming together of different religions.

A typical example of such usage is Dr Runcie's description of 'an ecumenical ashram' in India, 'where Roman Catholic,

Anglicans, members of the Church of North India and Hindus live and pray together'.[20]

IV

The above instances of the Laodicean interfaith compromise in this and the previous chapter are far from exhaustive. Examples abound and are increasing over the whole gamut of church life. On one level there is the church leader who in 1997 declared he was reading the Koran instead of the Bible during Lent.[21] On another level there is discussion amongst Church leaders about a multifaith service for the next coronation. In a magazine interview in 1997 the Archbishop of Canterbury was asked,

> 'Suppose that when his time comes to accede, Prince Charles were to say, "I want an interfaith coronation service." Would you be happy with that?'[22]

Dr Carey's reply showed that things were not clear cut. He said,

> 'I really must reserve my position on that, because it's so hypothetical. I don't mind being quoted that it's "No comment" ... I do not agree with interfaith worship. And other faiths don't like it either ... Assuming that establishment lasts, and I believe it will, it will inevitably be a Christian service.'[23]

And so we could go on, ad infinitum.

V

Interfaith compromise is deeply rooted throughout the whole body of the Church. Ruth Gledhill wrote in *The Times* that, 'increasing numbers of clergy in the Church of England embrace concepts of God that bear little relation to traditional Christianity but draw ideas from all the leading religions.'[24]

While it is to be hoped that very few Christians have gone so far as former members of the Nine O'Clock Service in Sheffield who celebrated the pagan service of Samhain in an Anglican Church,[25] interfaith events are being organised at the local church level.

In October 1998 the Canterbury Diocesan Spirituality Group organised a day on Buddhist Spirituality at the Franciscan Study Centre, Canterbury. This event was advertised in the diocesan newspaper, *Outlook*, and was described in an accompanying article as an 'opportunity to learn and practise Buddhist methods of prayer which many Christians are already using.'[26] Two such Christians were cited, namely Anthony de Mello, 'a Jesuit priest who used Hindu and Buddhist techniques in his ways to God', and Elaine MacInnes, 'a Zen master of world renown as well as a Roman Catholic nun.'[27]

The following month's edition of *Outlook* contained an account of a Christian-Buddhist Meditation Retreat at a Catholic pastoral centre. Amongst other things, the author said,

> 'We were led in the meditation taught by the Christian Meditation Centre, which involves the repetition of a mantra, and also in the two main Buddhist forms of meditation ... We also did Buddhist and Taizé chanting and listened to Christian and Buddhist teachings.'[28]

In this way light is mingled with darkness, and the resultant amalgam brought back to the local church, with dire consequences for all its members.

Many Christians are unwittingly caught up in the interfaith compromise. Those who practise Yoga and indulge in astrology are engaging with Hindu and New Age concepts. Our failure to witness to members of other faiths, or even to pray for their conversion, is a further mark of our unfaithfulness to the truth as it is in Christ.

Interfaith compromise seems to be peculiar to Christians. The Archbishop of Canterbury remarked in a speech to the General Synod of the Church of England that,

> 'I do not find that people of other faiths are clamouring to engage in multi-faith worship. Some of them have told me that they are puzzled by this apparent obsession amongst Christians.' [29]

It is we Christians who are throwing away the ultimate truth of our faith, even though our Scriptures warn us solemnly against such a thing. Multifaith compromise is our agenda. We are denying the truth of Jesus.

References

1. 'Communities and Buildings, A Report by the Inter-Faith Consultative Group of the General Synod Board of Mission', Church House Publishing, 1996, p. 16. Extracts from 'Communities and Buildings' are copyright © The Central Board of Finance of the Church of England, 1996; The Archbishops' Council, 1999 and are reproduced by permission.
2. J. Toy, *Cathedrals: Houses of God for all Nations*, Church Times 29.4.1994.
3. *ibid.*
4. 'Communities and Buildings', op.cit. p. 4.
5. *ibid.* p. 4.
6. *ibid.* p. 45.
7. *ibid.* p. 59.
8. *ibid.* p. 56.
9. *ibid.* p. 56.
10. *Church Times* 19.7.1996.
11. R. Runcie, *Christianity and World Religions*, p. 8.
12. *ibid.* p. 8
13. BBC 1, *Heart of the Matter*, 31.1.1991. Quoted in *Interfaith Update*, a leaflet published by the Open Letter Group.
14. *ibid.*
15. *Shalom*, the magazine of the Church's Ministry among the Jews, No. 3, 1998.

16. G. Carey, *Sharing a Vision*, Darton, Longman and Todd, 1993, pp. 178, 179.
17. Matthew 23:15; Acts 2:10; 6:5; 13:43. In the latter verse, the Greek word for 'proselytes' is rendered 'converts to Judaism.'
18. G. Carey, *Sharing a Vision*, p. 146.
19. *ibid*. p. 146.
20. R. Runcie, *One Light for One World*, SPCK, 1988, p. 193.
21. *Church Times* 14.2.1997.
22. *Third Way*, November 1997, p. 20.
23. *ibid*. p. 20.
24. *The Times* 16.2.1995. Copyright Times Newspapers Limited 1995.
25. *Church Times* 27.11.1998.
26. *Outlook*, Newspaper of the Diocese of Canterbury, September 1998.
27. *ibid*.
28. *Outlook*, October 1998.
29. G. Carey, *Sharing a Vision*, p. 243.

MARRIAGE

Chapter 12

Marriage Exalted

'And the Lord commanded us to do all these statutes,
to fear the LORD our God, for our good always.'
(Deuteronomy 6:24)

I

The Christian ideal of marriage is deep, pure and beautiful, and is neatly encapsulated in the scripture,

> *'Let marriage be held in honour among all, and let the marriage bed be undefiled.'* (Hebrews 13:4)

Here are two ingredients for a stable and lasting marriage, namely that it should be held in the highest regard, and that sexual activity must be kept within marriage. Neither cohabitation nor adultery is acceptable.

This teaching springs from the account of creation in Genesis, where God made both male and female (1:27), the woman being taken from the man (2:22), in order to be his helper (2:18). At the end of Genesis chapter 2 we have the definitive statement about marriage.

> *'Therefore a man leaves his father and his mother and cleaves to his wife, and they become one flesh.'*
> (Genesis 2:24)

God's ideal plan is for one man and one woman to join together in lifelong marriage. The man has to leave all other earthly relationships and be with his wife for ever. There can be no splitting apart, no breaking of the marriage bond. The married relationship is to be totally exclusive. The man and his wife become one flesh, which means they can enjoy a sexual relationship with each other, but with no one else. To seek sexual liaisons outside marriage is wrong, and destructive.

Within marriage there is a well defined role for both partners. In a real sense the man is the head of the woman. When God presented the newly created woman to the man, Adam named her saying,

> *'This at last is bone of my bones and flesh of my flesh; she shall be called Woman, because she was taken out of Man.'*
> (Genesis 2:23)

In Scripture to name someone implies authority over them.

Unlike Adam and the animals, who were created from the ground, the woman was created directly from the man, and was thereby part of him. Thus Adam could say she was *'bone of my bones and flesh of my flesh.'* Her name, woman, simply means *'she-man'*. She was of one nature with Adam, different only in sex.

Further, the woman was created from a rib, that is from the side of the man. This illustrates, in a beautiful way, the loving relationship between the two. As one Bible commentator puts it,

> 'The woman ... was not made out of his head to rule over him, nor out of his feet to be trampled upon by him, but out of his side to be equal with him, under his arm to be protected, and near his heart to be beloved.'[1]

Like all other aspects of human life, the institution of marriage was shattered after the Fall. The authority of the man turned into dictatorial dominance (Genesis 3:16), and both men and women indulged in sexual relationships outside marriage. Many of God's people failed to live up to His ideal, as the Old Testament makes abundantly clear. The philanderings of Judah (Genesis 38), the adultery of King David (2 Samuel 11), the voracious sexual appetite of Solomon (1 Kings 11:1–3) and the faithless wife in Proverbs 7, are four examples among many.

Yet throughout the Old Testament God continued to say that He had not altered His plan for marriage. The commandment, *'You shall not commit adultery'* (Exodus 20:14) emphasised the exclusive character of sex within marriage. God's mind about divorce was shown in the prophecy of Malachi.

> *'Let none be faithless to the wife of his youth. "For I hate divorce," says the* LORD *the God of Israel.'*
>
> (Malachi 2:15, 16)

Despite the sins of the people, marriage was always meant to be permanent and lifelong.

II

Jesus emphasised that God's ideal of marriage applied in all its fullness to those who followed Him. An incident recorded in Mark's gospel illustrates this. The Pharisees asked Jesus,

> *'Is it lawful for a man to divorce his wife?'*   (Mark 10:2)

Jesus responded,

> *'What did Moses command you?'*   (Mark 10:3)

The Pharisees answered,

> *'Moses allowed a man to write a certificate of divorce, and to put her away.'*   (Mark 10:4)

These words of Moses can be found in Deuteronomy 24:1–4. But Jesus looked at the reason for them and said,

> *'For your hardness of heart he wrote you this command-ment.'* (Mark 10:5)

In other words, Moses was coping with a situation which had grown up amongst sinful people.

Jesus then took the Pharisees back to God's original plan, and quoting Genesis said,

> *'... from the beginning of creation, "God made them male and female." "For this reason a man shall leave his father and mother and be joined to his wife, and the two shall become one flesh." So they are no longer two but one flesh.'* (Mark 10:6–8)

This led to the clear conclusion,

> *'What therefore God has joined together, let not man put asunder.'* (Mark 10:9)

As the Bible expositor, F.F. Bruce puts it,

> 'To the question, "Is it lawful for a man to divorce his wife?", His answer is, in effect, "No; Not for any cause." '[2]

God has joined a man and his wife together, and it is not for man to override the work of God.

The disciples of Jesus were either confused about the matter, or did not like what they heard, for,

> *'In the house the disciples asked Him again about this matter.'* (Mark 10:10)

If they expected a softening of the line, they were disappointed, because Jesus extended His teaching to include remarriage after divorce.

> *'Whoever divorces his wife and marries another, commits adultery against her; and if she divorces her husband and marries another, she commits adultery.'*   (Mark 10:11, 12)

Adultery is 'voluntary sexual intercourse between a married man or woman and a partner other than the legal spouse.'[3] So Jesus says the divorced person commits adultery because he or she is, in fact, still married to the first partner. Man-made divorce does not change anything. The original marriage still stands. Therefore, for the person who seeks to follow Jesus, marriage is always for life, and divorce is never an option. Even if the other partner has obtained a divorce, the divorced Christian is not free to remarry during the lifetime of his or her spouse.

Exactly the same teaching is given in Luke's Gospel.

> *'Everyone who divorces his wife and marries another commits adultery, and he who marries a woman divorced from her husband commits adultery.'*   (Luke 16:18)

Some verses in Matthew's Gospel have been used to claim that Jesus allowed divorce and remarriage on the grounds of the unfaithfulness of the wife. These verses, in the Revised Standard Version of the Bible, are as follows.

> *'It was also said, "Whoever divorces his wife, let him give her a certificate of divorce." But I say to you that every one who divorces his wife, except on the ground of unchastity, makes her an adulteress; and whoever marries a divorced woman commits adultery.'*   (Matthew 5:31, 32)

> *'And I say to you: whoever divorces his wife, except for unchastity, and marries another, commits adultery.'*
> (Matthew 19:9)[4]

The argument rages around the precise meaning of the word 'unchastity', which is a translation of the Greek word *porneia*. Some say *porneia* really means 'fornication', which is sexual uncleanness before marriage. Others believe it means 'incest', that is marriage within the prohibited degrees, and others claim that it means 'adultery'. This division of opinion finds its way into our Bible translations. The Authorised Version translates the word as 'fornication', the New King James Version as 'sexual immorality', whilst the Revised Standard Version and the New English Bible read 'unchastity'. The New International Version translates it as 'marital unfaithfulness', which is another way of saying adultery.

The following points, however, show that Jesus is not thinking of adultery, that is sexual sin committed **after** the marriage.

Firstly, the Greek words for 'to commit adultery' are *moicheuo* and *moichaoma*. These are used in a number of places in Matthew's Gospel with that meaning.[5]

Secondly, in Matthew 15:19, *moicheia* and *porneia* are listed as two separate sins, and not as the same thing.

Thirdly, if the husband divorced his wife on the grounds of adultery, he could hardly make her an adulteress, for she would be one already.

Fourthly, if Jesus was allowing any divorce it would mean that He was setting Himself against His Father, who hates divorce. It is inconceivable that Jesus would ever oppose His Father on this or any matter. As Jesus Himself said,

> *'I do nothing on my own authority but speak thus as the Father taught me.'* (John 8:28)

Therefore these verses do not give a fiat for the Christian to divorce, even in times of marital unfaithfulness. The teaching in these passages is no different from that given in Mark and Luke. Marriage is for life, and once entered cannot be dissolved, whatever the circumstances.

So we must ask what does Jesus mean by *'except for unchastity.'* There remain two alternatives, namely incest or sexual uncleanness before marriage. Both meanings of *porneia* are found in the Bible.

In 1 Corinthians 5 we have the instance of a man living with his father's wife, who is presumably his step-mother. Paul describes this in the following words,

> *'It is actually reported that there is immorality among you, and of a kind that is not found even among pagans; for a man is living with his father's wife.'*   (1 Corinthians 5:1)

The word translated 'immorality' in the RSV text is *porneia*, which therefore means incest. The couple are clearly living as man and wife, but they are not truly married for the so-called marriage is within the prohibited degrees.[6]

However, in John 8:41, *porneia* means premarital uncleanness. When Jews said to Jesus, *'We were not born of fornication'* (*porneia*) they were casting doubts on His parentage, and implying that His mother, Mary, had premarital sexual relations with some man other than her future husband, Joseph.

Thus, from biblical evidence, we can say that by *porneia* Jesus could have meant either incest or premarital sex. He could be saying that people who marry within the prohibited degrees are not married at all, or He could be talking about sex **before** marriage. In the latter case, He would be upholding the biblical precept that a man or woman belongs by nature to the first person with whom they have had sexual intercourse.[7] If a new husband found that his wife had had sexual relations with another man before the marriage, they were not married at all (Deuteronomy 22:13–21).

But whichever meaning Jesus had in mind, He is without doubt talking about a situation which existed **before** the supposed marriage, rendering it null. He is not referring to something which happened afterwards.

Rather than weakening Jesus' position concerning the impossibility of dissolving a marriage, these verses from the first Gospel actually uphold and strengthen it. They also show the importance of abstaining from sex before marriage.

The great importance Jesus gave to sexual purity is also seen in His remarks about lustful thoughts.

'You have heard that it was said, "You shall not commit adultery." But I say to you that every one who looks at a woman lustfully has already committed adultery with her in his heart.' (Matthew 5:27)

Like the physical act of adultery, inward lust is a serious matter, and extreme action has to be taken.

'If your right eye causes you to sin, pluck it out and throw it away; it is better that you lose one of your members than your whole body be thrown into hell.' (Matthew 5:28)

III

As we might expect, the teaching of Jesus is upheld in the rest of the New Testament.

Paul maintained that marriage is for life.

'To the married I give charge, not I but the Lord, that the wife should not separate from her husband (but if she does, let her remain single or else be reconciled to her husband) – and that the husband should not divorce his wife.'

(1 Corinthians 7:10, 11)

Even if the couple should separate, there can still be no divorce, for they remain married. The hope is that they may be reconciled. Failing this, they must live alone. This, Paul emphasised, was not his own teaching, but that of Jesus.

Once more the lifelong nature of marriage is emphasised. It cannot be broken by the decree of man, and everything must be done to make the marriage successful. The whole aim of counselling after a breakdown of relationships must be to bring the partners together again. No other way is possible for a Christian.

The church in Corinth had a problem in that some members were married to non-Christian partners. In advising on this matter Paul said,

'To the rest I say, not the Lord, that if any brother has a wife who is an unbeliever, and she consents to live with him, he should not divorce her. If any woman has a husband who is an unbeliever, and he consents to live with her, she should not divorce him. For the unbelieving husband is consecrated through his wife, and the unbelieving wife is consecrated through her husband. Otherwise, your children would be unclean, but as it is they are holy.'

(1 Corinthians 7:12–14)

The church in Corinth was no more than four or five years old when Paul wrote these words, and so it follows that most, if not all, of these mixed marriages had been contracted before either partner became a Christian.

Since the church members came from both Jewish and pagan backgrounds (Acts 18:1–11; 1 Corinthians 6:9), some of these marriages had no doubt been solemnised in pagan temples or by pagan rituals. Nevertheless Paul held that these couples were truly married. Therefore the Christian must not leave the non-believing partner, nor seek to break the marriage bond.

Paul encouraged obedience by showing the spiritual benefits which accrued through the Christian partner to the non-believing spouse, and to the children of the marriage. He also expressed the hope that by staying together, the Christian could win the spouse to Christ.

'Wife, how do you know whether you will save your husband? Husband, how do you know whether you will save your wife?' (1 Corinthians 7:16)

A similar thought is expressed by Peter in his first letter.

'Likewise you wives, be submissive to your husbands, so that some, though they do not obey the word, may be won without a word by the behaviour of their wives, when they see your reverent and chaste behaviour.'

(1 Peter 3:1, 2)

But what happens if the non-Christian partner wishes to separate? Paul taught,

> *'But if the unbelieving partner desires to separate, let it be so; in such a case the brother or sister is not bound. For God has called us to peace.'* (1 Corinthians 7:15)

This verse is known as the 'Pauline exception' or the 'Pauline privilege', and along with the verses from Matthew which have been considered above, is used by some to hold that in certain circumstances it is possible for Christians to divorce and remarry. However, if we look carefully at what Paul says, we shall find no exception to the rule of lifelong marriage.

The first part of the verse is clear and unambiguous. If the non-Christian partner of a marriage wishes to separate, then, in the end, the Christian must not stand in the way. He or she must allow the non-believing partner to opt out.

It is the phrase, *'not bound'* which causes a problem. Some say *'not bound'* indicates the Christian is not bound to the marriage itself, and is therefore free to remarry. Others affirm that even if the non-Christian separates the marriage still exists. Thus it does not indicate a change of status, but merely means the Christian should let the other party go their way.

A number of factors show that Paul does not mean that the marriage is over.

In the first place, the Greek word which we translate *'is not bound'* literally means 'is not enslaved' or 'is not under bondage'. It is a strong word which Paul never uses to describe the binding character of marriage. He uses a very different Greek word to say that marriage is lifelong, although this is not evident in our translations. [8]

In the second place, Paul says in the same chapter of Corinthians that,

> *'A wife is bound to her husband as long as he lives.'*
> (1 Corinthians 7:39a)

Therefore if he allowed remarriage after a pagan partner left he would be contradicting himself.

In the third place, Paul is not, in 1 Corinthians 7:15, talking about remarriage, but is giving practical advice about what to do if the non-believing partner wishes to separate. The severance, he says, must be peaceful, with as little rancour as possible. We have already seen that the best outcome of a separation is a subsequent reconciliation. It is obvious that the more anger at the time of separation, the less the likelihood of the couple coming together again. So Paul was giving good and sound practical counselling in the midst of a difficult situation, and was not in any way saying the Christian partner was free to remarry after the non-believer had separated.

There is, therefore, no Pauline exception. No matter what the non-Christian partner may do, the Christian is married for life, and may not remarry unless the first partner dies.

The marriage bond, in fact, is so strong and sacred, that Paul even compares it to the union between Christ and His Church. He says to Christian wives,

> *'Wives, be subject to your husbands, as to the Lord. For the husband is the head of the wife as Christ is the head of the church, His body, and is Himself its Saviour. As the church is subject to Christ, so let wives also be subject in everything to their husbands.'*   (Ephesians 5:22–24)

In similar manner he instructs Christian husbands,

> *'Husbands, love your wives, as Christ loved the church and gave Himself up for her, that He might sanctify her, having cleansed her by the washing of water with the word, that He might present the church to Himself in splendour, without spot or blemish or any such thing, that she might be holy and without blemish.'*   (Ephesians 5:25–27)

He then adds,

> *' "For this reason a man shall leave his father and mother and be joined to his wife, and the two shall become one*

flesh." This mystery is a profound one, and I am saying that
it refers to Christ and the church.'   (Ephesians 5:31, 32)

This gives a deep spiritual dimension to marriage. The bond between Christ and His Church is one of everlasting love, with Christ as the loving, self-giving head. The ideal is that a marriage reflects this love both in the way the partners relate to each other, and in the permanent nature of the union. It would be unthinkable for our Lord to renege on His promise never to leave us. In the same way it is impossible for a marriage to end in divorce.

Thus does the whole of the Bible bear witness to something which is clean and holy. God has given us marriage because He knows it is for our good. It is not an imposition from a remote deity, but the desire of a Father who loves us.

This is a treasure which God has entrusted to His Church. Although not everyone is called to be married, it is vital that we who are Christians uphold this sacred institution. In this way we help to bear witness to a bleeding and fractured world.

References

1. Matthew Henry, *Commentary on the Bible in One Volume*, ed. L.F. Church, Marshall, Morgan and Scott, 1960, p. 7.
2. F.F. Bruce, *The Hard Sayings of Jesus*, Hodder and Stoughton, 1983, p. 58.
3. *Collins Concise English Dictionary*, HarperCollins, 1992.
4. The Revised Standard Version points out some ancient variations of Matthew 19:9. Some old manuscripts after 'unchastity' read, 'makes her commit adultery', and some add at the end of the verse, 'and he who marries a divorced woman commits adultery'. The Authorised Version of the Bible incorporates the second of these alternatives into its text.
5. Matthew 5:27, 28, 32; 19:9, 18.
6. The word *porneia* actually occurs twice in 1 Corinthians 5:1. This is brought out in the Authorised Version, which is a more literal translation of the Greek. *'It is reported commonly that there is fornication among you, and such fornication as is not so much as named among the Gentiles, that one should have his father's wife.'*

7. Deuteronomy 22:28, 29 is one example of this teaching.
8. This point can be clearly seen by comparing the Greek word translated 'bound' in 1 Corintians 7:15 (*dedoulontai*), with that which Paul uses in Romans 7:2 and 1 Corinthians 7:39 (*dedetai*), where he says the wife is bound to her husband as long as he lives.

Chapter 13

Marriage Subverted

'Let your fountain be blessed,
and rejoice in the wife of your youth.'
(Proverbs 5:18)

I

It is a matter of common observation that marriage is increasingly held in dishonour. This can be seen in the lives of families, friends and neighbours, and in a vast array of statistics.

Fewer and fewer people are getting married. In 1995 there were 192,000 first marriages in the United Kingdom, which is half the 1970 total.[1] Of those married in 1995 only 45 per cent opted for a religious service, compared with 59 per cent in 1971.[2]

Cohabitation is now considered a viable alternative to marriage. The Office for National Statistics remarks,

> 'One of the main changes in family life over the last decade or so has been the fall in the proportion of people living in married couples and the increase in cohabitation.'[3]

In fact 'the proportion of all non-married women aged 18 to 49 who were cohabiting in Great Britain has doubled since 1981, to 25 per cent in 1996–7'.[4]

In tandem with fewer people getting married, the divorce rate in the United Kingdom has been steadily increasing. In 1961, for example, 0.23 per cent of married men were divorced. By 1992 the figure had risen to 1.37 per cent.[5]

Disregard of marriage has radically altered family life, and the last 25 years have seen a large growth of one parent families. In 1996 around 21 per cent of all families with dependant children were headed by a lone parent. This is nearly three times the 1971 figure.[6] Until the mid-1980s the majority of lone parent families were the result of divorce, but since then most of the increase has been caused by single lone mothers.[7] As is to be expected from these figures, the number of live births outside marriage has increased enormously over the past 25 years. In 1996, over one third of all such births in England and Wales were outside marriage, more than four times the proportion of 1971.[8]

It was not always thus. Well within living memory marriage was, on the whole, held in honour. Sex before marriage was deprecated, and those who chose to cohabit had to cope with the censure of society. The very phrase used to describe such cohabitation, 'living in sin', well expressed this attitude of disapproval.

Our present condition has not come to pass overnight. For many decades leading thinkers, writers and revolutionaries have sought to undermine, and even destroy, the institution of marriage. These voices reached a strident climax in the 1960s, when the concepts of free love and sexual liberation were openly espoused by the media and brought into every home in the land. Many ordinary people, who had little or no faith in God, soaked up and adopted such views.

Yet this style of living has not brought happiness or fulfilment. Behind the statistics of cohabitation, divorce and remarriage, are broken lives and deep hurts. Our so-called sexual liberation has left a trail of disturbed children and disillusioned people. In 1971 around 80,000 children under 16 were affected by their parent's divorce. By 1995 the figure had risen to just over 160,000.[9] It does not take much imagination to realise the damage to future generations. We live in a world where relationships are impure, selfish and unstable, always shifting, swapping and changing. Like Adam and Eve, we have become enmeshed in the bonds of self-made slavery.

II

There is a world of difference between the pure biblical teaching on marriage, and the deeply unsatisfying way of the world. Here, therefore, is a field where a distinctive Christian witness can be made. But once again we have compromised both our message and practice. Instead of leading the world, or even causing annoyance by speaking the truth, we are accepting the standards of society, and being sucked into the quagmire of immorality.

This is not a new phenomenon. For centuries the various branches of the Church have coped with the tension between upholding the biblical truth about marriage and divorce, and caring for members whose marriages have failed. Almost invariably the end-product has been an accommodation with the truth.

An early example of such a compromise is a ruling by Theodore of Tarsus, a 7th century Archbishop of Canterbury. He said,

'if a woman leave her husband, despising him, and will not return nor be reconciled to him, after five years and with the bishop's consent it shall be lawful for him to take another wife.' [10]

Down the ages the Protestant, Orthodox, and Roman Catholic churches have evolved schemes whereby members may, under certain conditions, remarry whilst their former spouse is still alive. The Protestant churches, generally speaking, accept divorce as pronounced by the state, and allow a divorced person to remarry in church.

Although claiming marriage to be indissoluble, the Orthodox Church also permits divorce and remarriage. It will not, however, accept a state divorce, but only one granted by the Church authorities. Based on an understanding (or misunderstanding) of the words of Jesus in Matthew 19:9,[11] such a divorce can in theory only be given on grounds of adultery, but in practice it is also granted on other grounds.[12]

The Roman Catholic Church approaches the problem in a different way. Whilst upholding the indissolubility of marriage, it has adopted the concept of nullity, and developed rules which allow the Church authorities to judge that certain unions have never been true marriages. Obviously such rules can be abused, leading to what amounts, in all but name, to divorce and remarriage within the Church.

The Church of England, as it emerged from the Reformation, differed from the rest of the Church by having a strict line on divorce and remarriage. It held that marriage was indissoluble, and could only be ended by the death of one partner. It 'knew nothing of divorce with liberty to remarry'.[13]

It is testimony to the Church of England's faithfulness that in the middle of the 20th century one writer could comment that it had,

> 'remained steadfast to these principles despite many temptations and encouragements to alter them.'[14]

III

As well as seeking to care for members whose marriages have broken down, the modern Church has to cope with living in an age of liberal attitudes to divorce and remarriage. Tremendous pressure has been, and still is, exerted on the churches to go along with the world, and this pressure has taken its toll across the whole Christian spectrum. The near collapse of the marriage discipline of the Church of England gives a bleak example of the present situation in the Christian community.

An early sign of emerging tension between the Church of England and the state came with the Matrimonial Causes Act of 1857. This Statute brought in easier divorce, with consequent freedom to remarry, by setting up a court with powers to grant divorce on grounds of adultery. Previous to this a divorce could only be obtained by Act of Parliament. The 1857 Act also stated that a Church of England incumbent could not be forced to solemnise a remarriage, but had to allow his church to be used for the same.

This meant that there was a clear division between the law of the state and that of the established Church. It also meant that if an incumbent wished to disobey Church law and remarry a divorced person, he could do so and claim the protection of the law of the land.

The Parliamentary debates on the Matrimonial Causes Act showed a division between leading members of the Church of England. The Act was vigorously opposed in the Commons by W.E. Gladstone, a leading lay Anglican, who held that marriage could not be dissolved. It was also opposed in the Lords by Bishop Wilberforce of Oxford, but the Archbishop of Canterbury and the Bishop of London gave it their support. From such divisions a full-blown compromise in the Church began to emerge.

An even clearer division was seen in 1909 during the deliberations of a Royal Commission on Matrimonial Law. Hensley Henson, then a Canon of Westminster, and later Bishop of Durham said,

'The absolute and uncompromising language (about the indissolubility of marriage) now common in Anglican circles is not really warranted either by the scriptures by which it is commonly justified, or by ecclesiastical history which is assumed to require it.'[15]

Cosmo Lang, the Archbishop of York and a member of the Royal Commission, took a very different line. In a minority report which he helped to write he held that the Commission's proposals to widen the grounds for divorce 'would

threaten the institution of family life.'[16] The fact that views
such as Hensley Henson's could be openly stated shows a
shift in the position of the Church of England, and a growth
of compromise with the teaching of the Bible.

During the first part of the 20th century the vast majority
of Anglican clergy remained faithful to the Church's position, and as late as the 1960s, 'the Church of England found
itself . . . to be the most rigorist of all Churches in its pastoral
practice in matrimonial cases.'[17]

Yet there was an increasing straining at the leash, and
there developed in the Church 'a widespread dissatisfaction
with the Church's existing discipline of marriage, and in
particular with its rule that 'no divorced person who has a
former partner still living may have a subsequent marriage
solemnised in church.'[18] This desire for change had nothing
to do with Christian truth, but with a Laodicean following of
the world.

In 1968 the Archbishop of Canterbury set up a Commission 'to prepare a statement on the Christian doctrine of
marriage.'[19] The introduction to the Commission's report
said that the statement,

> 'was to be prepared against the background of a debate
> in the Convocation of Canterbury "as to whether there
> might be occasions for relaxing the present rule of the
> Convocations whereby a divorced person with a former
> partner living may not have on remarrying a marriage
> service in church".'[20]

The Commission, known as the Root Commission after
its chairman Professor H. Root, presented its report in 1971,
and claimed that 'no certainty about the interpretation of
Jesus' sayings on remarriage can be attained'.[21] It also took
the line that the 'ecclesiastical regulations' (not scriptural
teachings be it noted) which discouraged the remarriage of
divorced people in church are based upon 'the moral
consensus of Christian people in the Church of England'.[22]
Therefore, it argued, so long as this moral consensus required

it, the present regulations should stay in place, but if it could be shown that the moral consensus had altered, the rules could then be changed. The report then suggested,

'it may well turn out on inquiry that a moral judgement on this matter has already formed itself within the Church of England, as it has in some other Churches of the Anglican Communion, in the belief that remarriage in church would not be a weakening but a strengthening of marriage.'[23]

Having built its house upon the sands of probabilities, the report concluded that if such a moral consensus was to be found,

'then it would be the duty of the Bishops-in-Synod to determine whether this consensus is theologically well founded. It is the unanimous conviction of this Commission that this is the case.'[24]

The Report closed with some suggestions as to when it would be in order to allow divorcees to be married in church. The teaching of the Bible, and the Church of England, was thus overturned to accord with the popular view of the day.

The Root report received a rough handling in the General Synod, and the Church's marriage discipline was not altered. Yet it was not too long before another Commission was set up, this time by the Archbishops of Canterbury and York in 1975, under the chairmanship of Bishop Skelton of Lichfield.

This Commission bit the bullet and by a majority in its report of 1978 recommended that,

'The Church of England should now take steps to revise its regulations to permit divorced people with the permission of the bishop to be married in church during the lifetime of a former spouse.'[25]

From then on things moved fast. In 1981 the General Synod passed a motion which said that there were circumstances in which the remarriage of a divorcee whose former spouse was still alive could be permitted. A scheme to regulate such marriages was put forward, but later withdrawn by the bishops after consultation within the dioceses. Some clergy opposed remarriage *per se*, and others did not like the proposed procedure to determine those eligible for remarriage in church. The bishops offered a revised procedure a year later, but this also met opposition and was withdrawn.

In 1985 a compromise was reached, which acknowledged the civil law right of the clergy to marry divorcees, but recommended that the bishops be consulted about such marriages. The result of this compromise was a massive breakdown in the marriage discipline of the Church.

The following figures for marriages in the Church of England and its sister church, the Church in Wales, show the extent of this collapse.[26]

Year	Number of marriages	Number of marriage involving at least one divorcee
1983	116,854	795
1988	118,423	5,529
1995	83,685	7,585

As a Working Party of the Ecclesiastical Law Society observed in its report on 'Marriage in Church after Divorce':

'It appears that the clergy are living with a familiar Anglican "fudge" and getting on with the job. It is difficult to estimate the proportion of clergy who regularly remarry those who have been divorced. Some who set out with the idea of remarrying a selected few have found it so difficult to administer in practice that they no longer do so ... Most lay people are thoroughly confused by the events of recent years, and many have little or no idea what the Church of England actually teaches or believes about marriage and divorce. Numbers of church-goers, as well as clergy, are unhappy not only about the principle of remarriage but also about the idea of their churches being used for that purpose.'[27]

In recent years influential voices in the Church of England have been pressing the Church to officially allow the remarriage of divorcees. In 1997 the Very Rev. David Edwards, Provost Emeritus of Southwark Cathedral, wrote in the foreword to the *Church of England Yearbook* that the Church should look again at working out a scheme to allow some second marriages. He remarked, in careful language, that,

> 'it can be argued by responsible theologians and pastors that the Church of England ought to resume its attempt to work out a careful procedure by which some second marriages could be authorised.'[28]

He also suggested that the Church should make available 'a process more in keeping with the Orthodox and main Protestant traditions and at least as compassionate as the provision for decrees of nullity in the Roman Catholic Church.'[29]

Whilst he admitted that divorce is 'one of the most devastating of the evils of our society',[30] the Provost used two approaches to push for remarriage of divorcees in the Church of England. The first was to suggest, as did the Root Commission, that because almost everybody else does it, so should we. As well as mentioning the Roman, Protestant and Orthodox traditions, he pointed out that 'official arrangements exist for Anglicans in Scotland and Ireland' to remarry in church after a divorce,[31] and that 'in England some priests already think it right to conduct some second marriages', and 'most . . . are usually willing to sponsor somewhat ambiguous blessings.'[32] He also gave his view that those who 'still think that all valid marriages are indissoluble before death' have probably become a minority within the Church.[33]

The second approach was the realignment of Scripture. The Provost wrote,

> 'the Church's Lord taught that the married ought to be one flesh until death.' [34]

In actual fact, the Church's Lord said that the married **are** one flesh until separated by death.

> *'They are no longer two but one flesh.'*   (Mark 10:8)

There is a world of difference between 'ought' and 'are'.

The Provost concluded that,

> 'the Sermon on the Mount allows divorce after adultery and St. Paul allows it after desertion by a non-Christian. Presumably the possibility of a new marriage is implied.' [35]

Our previous consideration of both Jesus' and Paul's teachings,[36] show that this is not the case.

Even as the Provost was writing, the Church of England was actively reviewing the whole matter. In 1995 the bishops had set up a Working Party to reconsider the Church's marriage discipline. The Working Party report entitled, *Marriage in Church after Divorce*, appeared in January 2000. It recommended that certain divorcees should be allowed to remarry in church.

The underlying nature of the report is seen in the first paragraph of the 'Summary of the Working Party's Approach.' It commences,

> 'We hold steadfastly to the view that marriage is a gift of God in creation and a means of grace and that it should always be undertaken as a lifelong commitment. Nothing in this report should therefore be taken to imply any change in the Church of England's teaching on marriage.' [37]

However, these words are totally negated by the subsequent sentences.

> 'We nevertheless believe that it can be said of two living people that they were married and are no longer married. We therefore concur with the General Synod's view (as expressed in 1981) that there are circumstances in which a divorced person may be married in church during the lifetime of a former spouse.'[38]

Two contradicting viewpoints are thus presented in one paragraph, and it is no surprise to find that the latter outlook decides the issue. The Report says its recommendations flow from its acceptance of the 1981 General Synod resolution, that

> 'there are circumstances in which a divorced person may be married in church during the lifetime of a partner.'[39]

In the following months the report was debated, and voted upon, by the diocesan synods of the Church of England. There was an overwhelming majority in favour of the principle that certain divorcees could be remarried in church, although many were unhappy about the proposed procedures for the same.

References

1. *Social Trends 28*, Office for National Statistics, Stationary Office, 1998, p. 50.
2. *ibid.* p. 49.
3. *ibid.* p. 48.
4. *ibid.* p. 48.
5. *Something to Celebrate*, A report of a Working Party of the Board of Social Responsibility of the General Synod of the Church of England, Church House Publishing, 1995, p. 35. It is too early to say whether a decrease in divorces, which was announced in 2001, is a harbinger of better times. It may simply reflect the fact that fewer people are getting married. Extracts from 'Something to Celebrate' are copyright © The Central Board of Finance of the Church of England, 1995; The Archbishops' Council, 1999 and are reproduced by permission.

6. *Social Trends*, p. 51.
7. *ibid.* p. 45.
8. *ibid.* p. 53.
9. *ibid.* p. 51.
10. Theodore, *Penitentiale*, XII.19, quoted in Latin in A.W. Haddon and W. Stubbs, *Councils and Ecclesiastical Documents*, Vol. 3, Oxford 1871, p. 200. The English version from J.R.H. Moorman, *A History of the Church in England*, Adam and Charles Black, 1963, p. 25.
11. See chapter 12, pp. 86–88.
12. T. Ware, *The Orthodox Church*, Penguin Books, 1967, pp. 301–2.
13. S.C. Carpenter, *Church and People 1789–1889*, SPCK, 1959, p. 340.
14. R. Haw, *The State of Matrimony*, SPCK, 1952, p. 180.
15. Royal Commission on Divorce and Matrimonial Causes, 1909. 'Minutes of Evidence', ii, p. 431. Quoted in J.L. Morgan, *A Sociological Analysis of Some Developments in the Moral Theology of the Church of England*, D.Phil. thesis, Oxford, 1976, p. 185.
16. *Something to Celebrate*, p. 24.
17. 'Marriage and the Church's Task', *The Report of the General Synod Marriage Commission*, CIO Publishing, 1978, p. 4. Extracts from 'Marriage and the Church's Task' are copyright © The Central Board of Finance of the Church of England, 1978; The Archbishops' Council, 1999 and are reproduced by permission.
18. *ibid.* p. 1.
19. 'Marriage Divorce and the Church', *The Report of the Commission on the Christian Doctrine of Marriage*, SPCK, 1971, p. xi. Extracts from 'Marriage Divorce and the Church' are copyright © The Central Board of Finance of the Church of England, 1971; The Archbishops' Council, 1999 and are reproduced by permission.
20. *ibid.* p. xi.
21. *ibid.* p. 94.
22. *ibid.* p. 71.
23. *ibid.* p. 71
24. *ibid.* p. 72.
25. *Marriage and the Church's Task*, p. 111.
26. *Marriage, Divorce and Adoption Statistics for 1983*, pp. 49, 51; for 1988, p. 51; for 1995, pp. 45, 47. Office for National Statistics, Stationary Office.
27. 'Marriage in Church after Divorce', Report of Working Party in *Ecclesiastical Law Journal*, vol. 2, pp. 359, 361. No copies may be made of this report without the permission of the Ecclesiastical Law Society.
28. David L. Edwards, 'Review of the Year 1996', *Church of England Yearbook 1997*, Church House Publishing, 1997, p. xxx. Extracts from 'The Church of England Yearbook, 1997' are copyright © The Central Board of Finance of the Church of England, 1997; The Archbishops' Council, 1999 and are reproduced by permission.

29. *ibid.* p. xxx.
30. *ibid.* pp. xxix, xxx.
31. *ibid.* p. xxx.
32. *ibid.* p. xxx.
33. *ibid.* p. xxx.
34. *ibid.* p. xxx.
35. *ibid.* pp. xxx, xxxi.
36. Chapter 12 pp. 86–88, 91, 92.
37. *Marriage in Church after Divorce*, Church House Publishing, 2000, p. xi. Extracts from 'Marriage in Church after Divorce' are copyright © The Archbishops' Council, 2000 and are reproduced by permission.
38. *ibid.* p. xi.
39. *ibid.* p. 50.

HOMOSEXUALITY

Chapter 14

Purity of Living

'You shall be holy; for I the LORD your God am holy.'
(Leviticus 19:2)

I

The Bible teaches that homosexual acts are always wrong.

As with all matters relating to sexual behaviour, the root of this teaching is found at the very beginning of the Bible, where it is seen that God's will for His people is lifelong marriage between one man and one woman.[1]

Two God-given laws specifically deal with homosexuality.

> *'You shall not lie with a male as with a woman; it is an abomination.'*   (Leviticus 18:22)

and,

> *'If a man lies with a male as with a woman, both of them have committed an abomination; they shall be put to death, their blood is upon them.'*   (Leviticus 20:13)

Two words, which appear in both laws, are particularly important. The first is 'male'. This word covers all ages. Homosexual acts are equally wrong whether they are committed by young people or by adult males. There can be no age of consent for such activity. The second word is 'abomination'. In Old Testament language this is a very strong word, reserved for sins such as idolatry, bestiality, child sacrifice, and occult involvement. Its use shows God's abhorrence of homosexual acts. This revulsion is reinforced by the prescription of the death penalty.

Other passages of Scripture send the same message. One such is the story of Lot in Sodom. As Lot entertained two angels, the men of the town surrounded his house and demanded that the angels, or men as they thought they were, be brought out, so that they could have sex with them.

> *'Bring them out to us, that we may know them.'*
> (Genesis 19:5)

The word 'know' in this context, as in many other places in the Bible, means to have a sexual relationship. The Sodomites were not seeking an introduction to the angels. They wanted to rape them. This is shown by the fact that Lot, perhaps in total panic, offered his daughters instead (Genesis 19:8). To his mind, the rape of his daughters was preferable to homosexual rape. Thankfully the angels had a better way of dealing with things, and Lot's whole family was spared.

The sin of homosexual lust and practice led to the destruction of Sodom. The New Testament letter of Jude speaks of

> *'Sodom and Gomorrah and the surrounding cities, which likewise acted immorally and indulged in unnatural lust.'*
> (Jude 7)

Because of this sin they underwent *'a punishment of eternal fire'* (Jude 7). Peter also mentioned these cities, and described the inhabitants as indulging *'in the lust of defiling passion'* (2 Peter 2:10). Indeed the name of Sodom has given rise to the word 'sodomy', a description of homosexual acts.

A similar story to that of Lot is found in Judges 19, where a traveller and his concubine spent the night in the Benjamite town of Gibeah. They were given hospitality by an old man of the town (verses 16–21), but some *'base fellows'* (verse 22) surrounded the house and said to the old man,

> *'Bring out the man who came into your house, that we may know him.'*   (Judges 19:22)

The old man pleaded with the crowd not to do *'so vile a thing'* (verse 24), and the traveller sent out his concubine, who tragically suffered mass rape and died (verses 25, 26).

Cult prostitution, which among other things included homosexual activity, is condemned in another passage of Scripture. Many of the nations around Israel indulged in such prostitution as part of the worship of their gods, but God told His people,

> *'There shall be no cult prostitute of the daughters of Israel, neither shall there be a cult prostitute of the sons of Israel. You shall not bring the hire of a harlot, or the wages of a dog, into the house of the LORD your God in payment for any vow; for both of these are an abomination to the LORD your God.'*   (Deuteronomy 23:17, 18)

Note that male cult prostitutes are described as dogs. This description is also found in some ancient Assyrian texts.[2]

Whenever the Jews became involved in pagan religions, cult prostitution, both male and female, raised its ugly head, and we read how three reforming kings, Asa, Jehoshaphat and Josiah, tried to get rid of the practice (1 Kings 15:12; 22:46 and 2 Kings 23:7).

II

When we turn to the New Testament we find that the unequivocal prohibition of homosexual acts is strengthened and underlined.

Although Jesus never explicitly mentioned homosexuality in His teaching, He made it clear that He upheld the whole

Jewish law, which, of course, included the laws against homosexual behaviour.

> *'Think not that I have come to abolish the law and the prophets; I have come not to abolish them but to fulfil them.'*
> (Matthew 5:17)

No law could be watered down or set aside.

> *'Whoever then relaxes one of the least of these commandments and teaches men so, shall be called least in the kingdom of heaven.'* (Matthew 5:19)

The Jewish Rabbis of the time said that homosexuality was not a problem amongst the Jews,[3] which may account for the silence of Jesus about this sin.

However, homosexual behaviour became a problem for the early Christians when the Church expanded into the Gentile world, where all kinds of homosexual acts were acceptable, and regarded as part of a young man's education. The Christian position was uncompromisingly based upon God's laws of the Old Testament. Paul, as apostle to the Gentiles, had most to say about the matter. His teaching was blunt and direct. He told the Corinthian Christians,

> *'Do not be deceived; neither the immoral, nor idolaters, nor adulterers, nor sexual perverts, nor thieves, nor the greedy, nor drunkards, nor revilers, nor robbers, will inherit the kingdom of God.'* (1 Corinthians 6:9, 10)

An echo of Paul's teaching in these verses is found at the end of Revelation, where John lists those who will be excluded from the heavenly Jerusalem.

> *'Outside are the dogs and sorcerers and fornicators and murderers and idolaters, and every one who loves and practises falsehood.'* (Revelation 22:15)

This refers back to Deuteronomy 23:18, where the term 'dogs' is used to describe male cult prostitutes.

Paul also refers to homosexual acts in 1 Timothy 1:9, 10. In these verses he enumerates sins which are *'contrary to sound doctrine'*, one of which is sodomy.

A more detailed mention of homosexual acts is found in Romans, chapter 1. In this chapter Paul looks at the pagan world as a whole, with all its evil and wickedness. Such a civilisation, he says, is under the wrath of God, because it refuses to worship Him, and turns instead to gods of its own making (verses 18–23). Therefore God has allowed the world to go its own way, and to end up in a cesspit of evil and vice (verses 24–32).

One particular vice which Paul mentions is homosexual behaviour, both gay and lesbian.

> *'For this reason God gave them up to dishonourable passions. Their women exchanged natural relations for unnatural, the men likewise gave up natural relations with women and were consumed with passion for one another, men committing shameless acts with men and receiving in their own persons the due penalty for their error.'*
>
> (Romans 1:26, 27)

Thus the whole witness of Scripture speaks with one voice. Homosexual acts are, without exception, sinful.

This does not mean that those who fall into such sins are eternally lost. God condemns the sin, with the sole aim of awakening sinners to their error, so that they may repent and be saved. The Gospel is about the salvation of sinners. In 1 Corinthians 6, after Paul has listed those who will not inherit the kingdom of God, he says with great joy to the Corinthian Christians,

> *'And such were some of you. But you were washed, you were sanctified, you were justified in the name of the Lord Jesus Christ and in the Spirit of our God.'*
>
> (1 Corinthians 6:11)

The church at Corinth had in its midst people who had been active homosexuals, thieves, robbers, drunkards and so on. But they had come to Jesus, confessed their sins, and were a new creation.

References

1. See chapter 12, pp. 82, 83.
2. G. Wenham, 'Homosexuality in the Bible, Sexuality and the Church', ed. T. Higton, *ABWON*, 1987, p. 28.
3. *ibid.* p. 33.

Chapter 15

The Justification of Sin

'On every side the wicked prowl,
as vileness is exalted among the sons of men.'
(Psalm 12:8)

I

Thirty or forty years ago most people regarded homosexual acts as sinful and to be avoided. Sadly the hatred of the sin often led to hatred of the sinner, and we Christians have much to confess in this respect.

However, the latter half of the 20th century has seen a radical change of attitude. Writing in the United States in 1948, Alfred Kinsey claimed in *Sexual Behaviour in the Human Male* that most males are by nature partly homosexual and partly heterosexual. He also asserted that about 4% of males are exclusively homosexual. In the United Kingdom a watershed was reached when the 1967 Sexual Offences Act decriminalised private homosexual sex for consenting adults over the age of twenty-one.

Nowadays homosexual activity, whether between two men or two women, is seen by many as an acceptable alternative to heterosexual behaviour, and sexual orientation is normally no barrier to obtaining employment. Gay and lesbian clubs and bars flourish openly, and well known people in all walks of life openly proclaim their homosexuality. This would have been unthinkable a generation ago.

As yet homosexuals do not have equal rights with heterosexuals, but Gay Rights activists are agitating for such parity. In 2000 the homosexual age of consent was reduced to sixteen, and there is now pressure to legalise homosexual 'marriages', or at least provide some legally binding arrangement for homosexual partners. The adoption of children by homosexual couples is another area of conflict, as is the bearing of children by lesbians, with donated sperm.

Acceptance of homosexuality is **worldwide**, and most countries are changing their laws in order to give more rights to homosexuals. We have therefore a clear distinction between what the world holds and what the Christian faith teaches.

Where does today's Church stand in all this? Has the truth, delivered once and for all, been faithfully guarded? Sadly it has not. Although many Christians have remained faithful to the truth, generally speaking the Body of Christ **has followed the world**. God's laws have been rejected by His people.

The progress of this compromise can be seen in the changing attitude of the Church of England. The story of four reports makes this clear.

II

The first report was published in 1954 by the Church of England Moral Welfare Council, and was entitled *The Problem of Homosexuality*. At that time most Christians would have believed the biblical teaching that all homosexual activity was immoral. However the Moral Welfare Council came up with what were, in those days, some revolutionary thoughts.

A distinction was drawn between those who were homosexual by nature, described as 'inverts', and those who were homosexual by nurture, described as 'perverts'. According to the report, the condition of inversion,

> 'is certainly due to psychological causes arising in adolescence and sometimes in early childhood, and may in some cases perhaps also be innate.'[1]

The pervert, however,

> 'is not a homosexual, but a heterosexual who engages in homosexual practices.'[2]

Although this distinction was presented as a matter of fact, it is debated even today, and cannot in any sense be said to be proven. The report also said that although homosexual practice was sinful, it should not be treated as illegal.

> 'The resultant inversion may be the result of psychological fixation. Such fixation ... will exempt an invert from responsibility for his homosexual condition but cannot absolve him from responsibility for immoral homosexual practices.'[3]

Copies of the report marked 'Private, not for publication', were sent, in the first place, to all members of both Houses of Parliament, but not to members of the Church Assembly, the forerunner of the General Synod.

Not all in the Church were happy with the report's conclusions. Some said it showed 'an excessive leniency towards the homosexual offender', and did not 'sufficiently emphasise the immorality and sinfulness of homosexual practices.'[4]

This report was the start of open compromise with the teaching of the Bible. The very fact that the Moral Welfare Council took the time to consider the so-called problem of homosexuality was in itself an act of compromise. As Eve looked upon the forbidden fruit, so the Council looked upon that which was forbidden by God.

The report had actually been initiated and drafted by the Rev. Dr Sherwin Bailey, who was the lecturer of the Moral Welfare Council. In 1955 he published a book *Homosexuality and the Western Christian Tradition* in which he claimed that the biblical teaching on homosexuality was irrelevant. He attempted to show that 'the Sodom story contains no reference to homosexual practices',[5] by saying that the men of Sodom merely wanted to get acquainted with Lot's visitors. Dr Bailey also claimed that the laws against homosexual behaviour in Leviticus were ambiguous, and merely stood 'as witness to the conviction shared by the ancient Hebrews with other contemporary peoples that homosexual practices are peculiarly disreputable.'[6] In other words they are not God's laws, but culturally conditioned taboos. Paul's explicit condemnation of homosexual sex in Romans 1 was dismissed as applicable only to perverts, and not to those who are homosexual by nature.

> 'Here then we have decisive Biblical authority for censuring the conduct of those whom we may describe as male perverts ... but do the Apostle's strictures apply also to the homosexual acts of the genuine invert, and in particular to those physical expressions of affection which may take place between two persons of the same sex who affirm they are "in love"? To such a situation it can hardly be said that the New Testament speaks, since the condition of inversion, with all its special problems, was quite unknown at that time.'[7]

III

The second report is known as the Gloucester Report, although its actual title is *Homosexual Relationships – a Contribution to Discussion*.

In 1974 the Principals of the Church of England Theological Colleges asked the Board for Social Responsibility (the successor to the Moral Welfare Council) for a Working Party to study 'the theological, social, pastoral and legal aspects of homosexuality.'[8] This was set up under the chairmanship of the Bishop of Gloucester. Its report was published in 1979, and included an open denial of the teaching of the Bible. The Bishop of Gloucester wrote in the Preface,

> 'We have not felt bound simply to repeat every utterance' (of Scripture).[9]

Rather,

> 'Accepting its authority as witness to the ways of God with men, and listening carefully to its teachings, we have at the same time laid claim, under the guidance of the Holy Spirit, to a liberty of judgement in discerning what God is saying to us here and now, whether it be something old or something new.'[10]

The body of the report took up the same theme, and contended that we have knowledge superior to that of the biblical writers. It held that Scripture merely reflected the views of a particular society at certain stages in their development. However,

> 'we live in a society which is in many ways very different from anything to be found in the Bible and we are often able to see a degree of relativity in biblical attitudes and standards, in a way that was not possible to previous generations, in the light of historical, anthropological, sociological and psychological knowledge which was not available to them.'[11]

Therefore, 'even when we can be confident that our text of the Bible is fixed and constant, the Church's understanding and use of it ... are not.'[12]

Having placed God under the authority of modern judgement, the conclusion was sadly predictable.

'There are circumstances in which individuals may justifiably choose to enter into a homosexual relationship involving the physical expression of sexual love.'[13]

This was such a radical departure from Christian teaching that the Board for Social Responsibility questioned whether to publish the report at all. They agreed to do so, but attached a report of their own, in which they made critical observations of the Working Party's conclusions. Thus two opposing views were issued together.

The resultant publication raised a storm of protest, although it had many defenders within the Church. A debate at the General Synod in 1981 furthered the confusion. Synod members were not allowed to vote for or against the report, and it was merely 'received'. This implied neither agreement nor disagreement.

IV

In 1986 the bishops commissioned yet another report on homosexuality. The aim of this report was 'to guide and assist the thinking of the House of Bishops'.[14] Once again the Board for Social Responsibility set up a Working Party, this time under the chairmanship of the Rev. June Osbourne. The Working Party had seven members, and the report, known as the Osbourne Report, expressed their unanimous opinion.

An aura of secrecy has always surrounded this document. The Working Party was told to report in strictest confidence to the House of Bishops. Although the bishops refused to publish the Report, copies were leaked, and it is known that it contained a whole series of highly radical opinions and comments, which bore no resemblance to traditional Christian teaching.

According to one publication the Osbourne Report justified physical homosexual relationships. Although it accepted that

there is strong biblical disapproval for homosexual practice, it
declared that,

> 'it might be judged that loving, committed and trusting
> relationships between homosexual people, whilst in
> some respects they are considered sinful and falling
> short of the pattern of our life as revealed in Scripture,
> make the best moral sense of a situation which is, in
> itself, flawed.' [15]

In addition the Report allegedly discussed services for the
blessing of homosexual couples.

> 'More work needs to be done on the question of services
> of blessing for such couples and whether it could be
> right for the church officially to encourage such a
> practice. Many Christians would be unable to endorse
> such practices. Others believe that the way forward
> would be to allow quiet private arrangements to be
> made with co-operative clergy.' [16]

Once more we are back in Laodicea. If homosexual
relationships are declared sinful in Scripture, as the Report
is claimed to have admitted, there cannot be any justification
for blessing them. How can we bless that which God calls an
abomination?

It was little wonder that the secular press had a field day.
Here was a report from within the Church, which challenged
the Church's own teaching. The fact that it was meant to be a
private report only added piquancy to the situation.

V

The fourth report was issued by the House of Bishops in
December 1991, and was entitled *Issues in Human Sexuality*.

The Laodicean nature of this report is seen in its second
paragraph, which says that the report is,

'no more than one stage in a discussion which needs to be continued throughout the Church by individuals and groups who learn humbly and prayerfully to be open to facts, to one another, and to Scripture, Tradition and reasoned reflection on experience.' [17]

This implies that the discussion could go to other stages. Such an implication must be rejected by those who hold to the biblical teaching. God has spoken and His Word stands for all time. We cannot discuss it, as though it could be altered by human wisdom or democracy.

It is interesting to note that the report made special mention of the much maligned Osbourne Report. The authors say,

'We wish to put on record here our gratitude for the help this Report has given us.' [18]

They additionally tell us that 'we have also had the help of gay and lesbian Christians who have generously shared with us their own experiences and concerns.' [19] Instead of looking solely to the Lord and His Word and seeking guidance from above, guidance has been sought from below.

It is not hard to anticipate the conclusions of this report. On the one hand we are told that homosexual acts,

'do not constitute a parallel and alternative form of human sexuality as complete within the terms of the created order as the heterosexual'. [20]

But on the other hand we are asked to believe that homosexual relationships are permissible for lay members of the Church. Whilst some Christian homosexuals feel called to follow the path of sexual chastity,

'at the same time there are others who are conscientiously convinced that this way of abstinence is not the best for them, and that they have more hope of growing in love for God and neighbour with the help of a loving and faithful homophile partnership, in intention life-long, where mutual self-giving includes the physical expression of their attachment.'[21]

The bishops add 'we do not reject those who sincerely believe' that homosexual physical expression 'is God's call to them. We stand alongside them in the fellowship of the Church, all alike dependent upon the undeserved grace of God.'[22]

Yet what was allowed for lay people was denied to the clergy.

'In our considered judgement the clergy cannot claim the liberty to enter into sexually active homophile relationships.'[23]

This is inconsistent. How can a moral law be right for one group and wrong for another? Surely God's Word is true for all.

The report brought criticism from all parts of the Church of England. Those who held to traditional teaching said it was heretical, whereas others claimed it did not go far enough. A debate in the General Synod in July 1997 resulted in the report being commended for discussion, prayerful study and reflection in the dioceses, deanery synods, clergy chapters and congregations of the Church of England. This meant that the Church as a whole was called upon to look at forbidden fruit, and to pass judgement on the Word of God.

VI

These reports mark a compromise which has spread throughout the whole Church of England. Its widespread nature can be seen in many places.

The extension of the word 'family' to include cohabiting homosexuals, is common practice in official circles. Thus a work on the family, entitled *Something to Celebrate*, published in 1995 by the General Synod Board of Social Responsibility talks about 'gay and lesbian families'.[24] The authors suggested that such families 'ought to find a ready welcome within the whole family of God'.[25]

Clearly such a welcome involves the acceptance of the sinful nature of such unions, without a challenge to repent.

> 'We are also aware of the gifts which lesbian and gay families have to offer to the Church and to the wider community and of the particular perspectives lesbian and gay people may have on human relationships.'[26]

The twentieth anniversary service of the Lesbian and Gay Christian Movement in 1996 showed the same compromise. Not only was the service held in Southwark Cathedral, but both the bishop of the diocese and the provost of the cathedral were present. The preacher was a bishop who had been a member of the group which drew up the Osbourne report. The presence of such leading churchmen gave a clear indication as to how far the Church had accepted homosexual practice. This service was not simply a one-off. A year later the Birmingham branch of the Lesbian and Gay Christian Movement held its 10th anniversary service in Birmingham, and again the preacher was a bishop. In February 1999 the Lesbian and Gay Christian Movement held a conference in Derby. Of the 270 people attending, 12 were serving bishops.[27]

Two further signs of the times are pressures from within the Church to ordain openly active homosexuals,[28] and the publication in diocesan magazines and newspapers of advertisements from the Lesbian and Gay Christian Movement.

This compromise is not just within the Church of England. Other Anglican churches are moving along the same path, and some, such as the Episcopal Church in the United States, have moved much further.

Other denominations, such as the Methodists and the United Reformed Church, are deeply tainted with this compromise. The Uniting Church in Australia (a merger of Congregational, Methodist and Presbyterian churches) published a report in May 1996, which recommended that the Church should consider covenantal services for homosexual unions, and should accept and approve of already existing homosexual partnerships.[29]

There is, of course, considerable opposition within the churches to any acceptance of homosexual behaviour. The General Synod of the Church of England held a debate on homosexuality in 1987, and apparently reaffirmed the biblical teaching on sexual matters, although some thought the outcome was inconclusive. In recent years various Anglican leaders have expressed deep concern. A group of bishops from the southern hemisphere issued what is known as the Kuala Lumpur Statement, which reaffirmed traditional Christian teaching on sexual matters, and in 1998 the Anglican bishops at the Lambeth Conference declared homosexual practice to be 'incompatible with scripture', and advised against 'legitimising or blessing same sex unions' or 'ordaining those involved in same gender unions.'[30]

Nevertheless, the compromise grows and threatens to overwhelm the Church. Instead of offering a Gospel which can change our sinful nature, we are accepting sin on its own terms. The situation is very serious.

References

1. 'Sexual Offenders and Social Punishment', Appendix III (Extracts from *The Problem of Homosexuality*), Church Information Board, 1956, p. 103. Extracts from 'Sexual Offenders and Social Punishment' are copyright © The Central Board of Finance of the Church of England, 1956; The Archbishops' Council, 1999 and are reproduced by permission.
2. *ibid*. p. 104.
3. *ibid*. p. 106.
4. *ibid*. p. 4.
5. D. Sherwin Bailey, *Homosexuality and the Western Christian Tradition*, Longman, Green and Co., 1955, p. 8.

6. *ibid.* p. 156.

7. *ibid.* p. 157.

8. *Homosexual Relationships – a Contribution to Discussion*, Church Information Office Publishing, 1979, p. 3. Extracts from 'Homosexual Relationships – a Contribution to Discussion' are copyright © The Central Board of Finance of the Church of England, 1979; The Archbishops' Council, 1999 and are reproduced by permission.

9. *ibid.* p. 4.

10. *ibid.* p. 4.

11. *ibid.* p. 33.

12. *ibid.* p. 33.

13. *ibid.* p. 67.

14. *Issues in Human Sexuality*, Church House Publishing, 1991, p. 2. Extracts from 'Issues in Human Sexuality' are copyright © The Central Board of Finance of the Church of England, 1991; The Archbishops' Council, 1999 and are reproduced by permission.

15. *ABWON News*, Spring 1995, p. 2.

16. *ibid.* p. 2.

17. *Issues in Human Sexuality*, p. 1.

18. *ibid.* p. 2.

19. *ibid.* p. 4.

20. *ibid.* p. 40.

21. *ibid.* p. 41.

22. *ibid.* p. 41.

23. *ibid.* p. 45.

24. *Something to Celebrate*, p. 120.

25. *ibid.* p. 120.

26. *ibid.* p. 120.

27. *Church Times* 12.2.1999.

28. See chapter 21, pp. 181–184.

29. *Church Times* 14.6.1996.

30. *Church Times* 21.8.1998.

MONEY

Chapter 16

Money Matters

*'Honour the LORD with your substance
and with the first fruits of all your produce;
then your barns will be filled with plenty,
and your vats will be bursting with wine.'*
(Proverbs 3:9, 10)

I

'Ladies and gentlemen', boomed a stentorian voice, 'the draw is about to be made.'

All activity ground to a halt, and everyone looked expectantly towards the platform. A local worthy stepped forward, and drew out the first number. St. Agatha's Autumn Fayre had reached its climax.

A typical scene from a church fund raising event. But is this the right way? No one would deny that the Church needs money. It has buildings to heat, light, insure and maintain. Most churches have full-time ministers who have to be paid. Also any church worth its salt tries to help those in need.

The real question is, how is the necessary finance to be raised? The Christian answer is simple and profound. All money required for the church comes through the sacrificial giving of God's own people.

II

The Jews of the Old Testament had two sacred buildings. The first was the portable tabernacle, which was built in the wilderness, and the second was the Jerusalem temple, which replaced the tabernacle in the days of King Solomon.

When God commanded the Israelites to build the tabernacle and make sacred vestments for the priests, He decreed that the materials were to be given by the Israelites themselves.

> *'The Lord said to Moses, "Speak to the people of Israel, that they take for me an offering; from every man whose heart makes him willing you shall receive the offering for me. And this is the offering which you shall receive from them: gold, silver, and bronze, blue and purple and scarlet stuff and fine twined linen, goat's hair, tanned ram's skins, goatskins, acacia wood, oil for the lamps, spices for the anointing oil and for the fragrant incense, onyx stones, and stones for setting, for the ephod and for the breastpiece. And let them make me a sanctuary, that I may dwell in their midst." '*
>
> (Exodus 25:1–8)

Moses relayed these instructions to the people, who obeyed with a generous spirit (Exodus 35), bringing far more than was required (Exodus 36:2–7). This giving was a freewill offering. There was no compulsion. The materials were to come from *'every man whose heart makes him willing'* (Exodus 25:2), or as Moses put it, from *'whoever is of a generous heart'* (Exodus 35:5).

After the tabernacle had been built, the upkeep was provided by a tax of half a shekel, payable by all Israelites over the age of twenty (Exodus 30:12–16). The principle of God's people providing for God's work held good.

The building of the Jerusalem temple was also financed through the giving of the Israelites. In a great outpouring of generosity, the elderly King David and the leaders of the people made freewill offerings of money and materials, so that Solomon could build the temple (1 Chronicles 29:1–9).

The half shekel tax continued to be levied after the temple had been built, and became known as the temple tax. We have a record of it being used in the reign of king Joash to finance various repairs to the temple (2 Chronicles 24:1–14; 2 Kings 12:1–18). This tax was still collected in the days of Jesus, and was paid by our Lord Himself (Matthew 17:24–27).

III

Turning now to the ministry, we read in the Old Testament that the full-time Levitical priesthood was financially supported by the tithe.

The Lord said that a tithe, that is a tenth of everything, belonged to Him.

> *'All the tithe of the land, whether of the seed of the land or of the fruit of the trees, is the LORD's; it is holy to the LORD … And all the tithe of herds and flocks, every tenth animal of all that pass under the herdsman's staff, shall be holy to the LORD.'*   (Leviticus 27:30, 32)

Each Israelite family had an obligation to give one tenth of its income to the Lord. Once given, the tithe was used to provide material support for the priests, who had *'no inheritance among the people of Israel'* (Numbers 18:24).

> *'To the Levites I have given every tithe in Israel for an inheritance, in return for their service which they serve, their service in the tent of meeting.'*   (Numbers 18:21)

The priests also had to give a tithe, which was known as a tithe of a tithe. This was used to support the high priest (Numbers 18:25–28).

The tithe was to be used exclusively for the priesthood. Other causes for which money was required had to be met by offerings over and above the tithe. Thus the Old Testament talks about tithes **and** offerings (Malachi 3:8). They were different accounts, used for different purposes.

The New Testament Church also had a full-time ministry, and the principle of giving by God's people still applied. Jesus Himself *'commanded that those who proclaim the gospel should get their living by the gospel'* (1 Corinthians 9:13, 14). He put this into practice when He sent out the seventy (Luke 10:1–12), and told them that if they were accepted in a house, they had to remain there,

> *'eating and drinking what they provide, for the labourer deserves his wages.'* (Luke 10:7)

Since Jesus upheld the whole law, it follows that He accepted the need to tithe. He mentioned this practice in the midst of berating the Pharisees.

> *'But woe to you Pharisees! for you tithe mint and rue and every herb, and neglect justice and the love of God.'* (Luke 11:42a)

He did not say that the Pharisees should stop tithing and concentrate on justice and the love of God, but that they should do both.

> *'These you ought to have done, without neglecting the others.'* (Luke 11:42b)

In like manner Paul wrote to the church in Corinth,

> *'Do we not have the right to our food and drink? ... Who serves as a soldier at his own expense? Who plants a vineyard without eating any of its fruit? Who tends a flock without getting some of the milk? ... If we have sown spiritual good among you, is it too much if we reap your material benefits?'* (1 Corinthians 9:4, 7, 11)

The fact that Paul chose not to accept the support of the Church (1 Thessalonians 2:9), in no way obviated the principle. God's ministers should be financially supported by God's people, it was their *'right in the gospel'* (1 Corinthians 9:18).

IV

God's people were also required, at their own expense, to care for the poor in their midst.

In the Old Testament God instructed His people about the perpetual problem of poverty, and of their personal responsibility to the poor.

> *'For the poor will never cease out of the land; therefore I command you, You shall open wide your hand to your brother, to the needy and to the poor, in the land.'*
>
> (Deuteronomy 15:11)

Thus the farmer must neither bring in all his harvest, nor gather up the gleanings, but leave them for the poor (Leviticus 19:9, 10), and an Israelite could not charge interest on a loan to a poor fellow Jew (Exodus 22:5).

Echoing Deuteronomy Jesus taught His followers to care for the poor.

> *'For you always have the poor with you, and whenever you will, you can do good to them.'*   (Mark 14:7)

Support for the poor had to come from church members. The apostle John taught,

> *'If any one has the world's goods and sees his brother in need, yet closes his heart against him, how does God's love abide in him?'*   (1 John 3:17)

The same principle is found in Paul's instructions regarding a collection for the poverty-stricken Jerusalem Christians. He wrote to the church in Corinth,

'Now concerning the contribution for the saints: as I directed the churches of Galatia, so you also are to do. On the first day of every week, each of you is to put something aside and store it up, as he may prosper, so that contributions need not be made when I come.' (1 Corinthians 16:1, 2)

Paul stressed in 2 Corinthians 8 and 9 that this collection was a free will offering. No level of giving was mentioned. It was left to the individual Christian to give as he prospered.

The same emphasis on personal giving is found in Paul's comments on work.

'Let the thief no longer steal, but rather let him labour, doing honest work with his hands, so that he may be able to give to those in need.' (Ephesians 4:28)

The Church's care for its widows (Acts 6:1–6; 1 Timothy 5:3–16) and for its members who were suffering from famine (Acts 11:27–30), are good examples of the Christian community caring for its poor according to biblical precepts.

Thus the basic principle holds good throughout the whole of the Bible. The money required for every facet of God's work has to come from God's people.

V

Christian giving is a matter of faith in God. In order to encourage us in this faith, both Old and New Testaments show that if we are generous with what we have, God will care for us in ways beyond our expectations.

One of the great names of God in the Old Testament is *Jehovah-jireh*, which means 'the Lord will provide'. This name was used by Abraham after the Lord had provided a ram for sacrifice in the place of his son Isaac (Genesis 22:14). As Abraham had been willing to give up his most prized possession, so those who are willing to give sacrificially will be cared for by the Lord.

In the days of Malachi, the Jews were failing to pay the full tithe. Speaking through the prophet, God says this is robbing Him of His due.

> *'Will a man rob God? Yet you are robbing me. But you say, "How are we robbing Thee?" In your tithes and offerings. You are cursed with a curse, for you are robbing me; the whole nation of you.'*   (Malachi 3:8, 9)

Therefore the people are bidden,

> *'Bring the full tithes into the storehouse, that there may be food in my house.'*   (Malachi 3:10a)

This command is immediately followed by a promise.

> *'Thereby put me to the test, says the LORD of hosts, if I will not open the windows of heaven for you and pour down for you an overflowing blessing.'*   (Malachi 3:10b)

The story of Elijah and the widow of Zarephath, whose oil never ran out, is just one illustration of this certainty of faith (1 Kings 17:8–16).

Paul showed the same trust in God when encouraging the Corinthian Christians to give to the poor saints in Jerusalem. He told them,

> *'The point is this: he who sows sparingly will also reap sparingly, and he who sows bountifully will also reap bountifully ... God is able to provide you with every blessing in abundance, so that you may always have enough of everything and may provide in abundance for every good work.'*   (2 Corinthians 9:6, 8)

Paul added a new and deeper dimension to Christian giving, by linking it to the sacrifice of Jesus.

'For you know the grace of our Lord Jesus Christ, that though He was rich, yet for your sake He became poor, so that by His poverty you might become rich.' (2 Corinthians 8:9)

Jesus was willing to let go of all the riches of heaven and come to earth to be our Saviour. By His sacrifice, consummated in the Cross, He brought the richness of eternal life to all who would believe, and Himself entered into everlasting glory. Thus if we would truly follow Him and partake of His life, we must be willing to sacrifice our worldly riches for the sake of others, in complete faith in God who provides for all our needs. This is the Christian way of giving.

Chapter 17

The Sacrifice of Giving

'I will not offer burnt offerings to the Lord my God
which cost me nothing.'
(2 Samuel 24:24)

I

Although many churches use bring and buy sales, jumble sales, Autumn Fayres and the like, to raise money, it is not hard to see that such events are far from scriptural, and are based on worldly ideas and methods.

Some churches do follow the biblical teaching, and there are many stories of true sacrificial giving.

In his book *The Sunderland Refreshing* Ken Gott relates how the Sunderland Christian Centre set about financing a new place of worship in the early 1990s. The initial cost for the project was £500,000, and the church eldership of five men committed themselves to giving £10,000 each. This meant, for some, selling their homes and buying cheaper property. Other church members followed suit, with the result that the necessary bills were met.

> 'Supernaturally the congregation just kept giving and giving over and over again, with none of us really knowing where the money had come from. We never received a grant or large gift from outside of the fellowship ... We

never missed a deadline for paying the contractors, though we were often right up against it. We would have a bill to meet by Monday morning and would simply pray the money in. On one Sunday morning £12,000 came in the offering – and that was over and above the normal giving to the church.'[1]

As in Sunderland, so in Bradford, where at a special service in 1998 the members of the Abundant Life Church gave or promised £600,000 towards the cost of a new church centre. The church banned all sponsoring and fund raising efforts and used the motto, 'Equal Sacrifice not Equal Giving'. This meant that the entire sum came from the church family. Some sold cars, one member cashed in an insurance policy and raised £8,000, another sold shares for £7,000. The leaders of the church gave £160,000 between them, and about 100 children pooled their pocket money to give £1,000.[2]

II

Various money-raising events, such as raffles and bingo sessions, involve gambling. This is a sinful activity which should have no place in the Body of Christ. The motivation of gambling is greed and covetousness. This breaks the commandment, *'You shall not covet'* (Exodus 20:17), and undermines any attempt by the Church to encourage pureness of living. A church which gambles is working against itself. Jesus told us,

> *'Take heed, and beware of all covetousness; for a man's life does not consist in the abundance of his possessions.'*
> (Luke 12:15)

He also said, *'a divided household falls'* (Luke 11:17). Every time the Body of Christ indulges in gambling it is actively encouraging its members to sin, thus effecting its own destruction.

Further, gambling always leads to inequality of wealth. Many pay in, but few draw out. This is in direct opposition to the purpose of Christian giving. Paul teaches that giving to the poor is *'a matter of equality'* (2 Corinthians 8:14). He writes,

> *'Your abundance at the present time should supply their want, so that their abundance may supply your want, that there may be equality.'*   (2 Corinthians 8:14)

Gambling is rooted in paganism, where it is held that the gods direct the dice or the cards. The winners are favoured by the gods and the losers are in divine disfavour. We come across this when we talk loosely about Lady Luck, or the luck of the draw.

Some Christians gamble to support good causes. Yet in most cases only part of the cost of a raffle or lottery ticket goes to charity. It is, in any case, more blessed to give without any thought or hope of receiving (Acts 20:35).

There is mention in the Scripture of the sacred lot. This consisted of two stones, or similar objects, known as Urim and Thummim, which were placed in the breastpiece of the high priest (Exodus 28:30). The purpose of the lot was to discover the will of God in certain situations. Recorded examples of its use include the choosing of one of two goats for sacrifice on the Day of Atonement (Leviticus 16:8), and the division of the land of Canaan amongst the twelve tribes of Israel (Numbers 26:55). It was also employed to discover who had disobeyed a command of King Saul (1 Samuel 14:24–46). Since it was used to find God's will, and not for covetous gain, the sacred lot does not, in any way, imply God's approval of gambling.

III

The advent of the National Lottery has taken us deeper into the sin of gambling. When introducing the Lottery the Government said its 'whole purpose is to benefit good causes and to help to improve the quality of life for people in this country.'[3] Since its introduction at the end of 1994, millions of pounds have been distributed to many and varied causes.

However, from the biblical viewpoint, the National Lottery cannot be conscientiously supported by Christians. This position was spelled out by the Anglican Bishop of St. Albans during the second reading of the National Lottery Bill in the House of Lords. Despite there being general agreement in that House for the principle of the Bill, the bishop firmly stated,

'I deplore the Government's decision to go down this path. I do not believe it to be right.'[4]

He then expressed three anxieties about the Lottery. These were 'that there is something implicity deceitful about the state encouraging people to part with their money through the enticement of personal gain in order to spend the proceeds on matters which should be funded more properly from the public purse';[5]; that 'a national lottery, by virtue of its scale, will undermine the whole idea of charitable giving';[6]; and that 'I am uneasy about the whole idea of the state formally endorsing gambling ... Some will be tempted above their means with all the consequences that that may entail for their lives and those of their families.'[7]

Finally, the bishop sounded a specifically Christian note.

'Many in the Churches, like myself, will be saying to their congregations "Do not put your money in the lottery basket. Do not be seduced either by the siren voices which tell you that it is all for a good cause when you know that only £1 out of £4 is going to that good cause. And do not be seduced by the greedy voice inside you ... which says that you may be one of the lucky ones and strike it rich." For years now the Churches have tried to discourage that particular temptation and have deplored raising money through the typical church raffle or tombola stall. Our teaching is that you must give. The Churches insist and demand that people give. It is the teaching of Christ to give. Giving is good for you. But this is a poor second best which it is wise to avoid.'[8]

In all this the bishop was being faithful to the official Church of England position, as enunciated by the old Church Assembly. In 1932, as a response to a Royal Commission on Gaming and Lotteries, the following resolution had been passed,

'That this Assembly views with grave anxiety the great evils caused by betting and gambling, and earnestly hopes the Royal Commission now sitting may devise effective means of checking incitements to betting and the exploitation of the gambling instinct for private profit or for charitable institutions.'[9]

This resolution was reaffirmed by the Assembly in 1950.[10]

The National Lottery was officially described as a reaction 'to a perfectly natural inclination of most human beings periodically to want to have a bit of a flutter'.[11] In other words, it encourages the gambling instinct. As well as being used for the benefit of charities, it exploits the gambling instinct for state and private profit. As such it falls foul of the position of the Church Assembly. So we would expect the Church of England, and indeed all Christian churches, to have nothing to do with it.

Sadly, this has not proved to be the case. Many individual church leaders have criticised the Lottery. The Anglican Bishop of Liverpool, for example, described it as an 'evil genie let out of the bottle.'[12] Yet in a statement of January 1995 the Church of England bishops adopted a position of total compromise. Whilst criticising the Lottery as 'a form of nationally sponsored gambling designed to encourage false hopes and over-indulgence',[13] and declaring that, 'we see no basis on which lottery money should be used by the Church' in the areas of 'worship, witness, evangelism and pastoral care',[14] they indicated a willingness to take Lottery money for maintaining historic church buildings. It was argued that 'the repair and maintenance of its historic churches and cathedrals and the upkeep of its historic archives and other artefacts are responsibilities which the Church of England undertakes in part on behalf of the nation as a whole',[15] and therefore some would think it right to apply for Lottery funds for this purpose.

> 'Sometimes, the Church resists proposed changes in our society, but when the decision is made we have to live with it. In this instance, we recognise that the Government has made clear that the lottery is the way in which it will increasingly fund heritage and charitable and other matters. The Church will continue to need help from the nation in maintaining its large part of the national heritage and it seems inevitable that help from the public funds raised through the lottery will be seen by some parishes and others as necessary in fulfilling their share in that responsibility. Some Church organisations will also decide to draw on the funds raised by the lottery for charitable work.'
>
> 'The decision whether or not to apply for such help is a matter for the responsible body in each case. A decision to apply should not be seen as lessening the criticisms the Church has about the lottery, or about the nation's heritage and other worthy causes being supported by this as opposed to other sources of public funding.'[16]

Unlike the Church of England, the Church of Scotland initially refused to accept Lottery money. In 1994 its General Assembly declared that 'participation in the National Lottery would be contrary to the Church's position opposing gambling in all its forms.'[17] Accordingly, a year later, the Assembly declined to accept money from the Lottery for any purpose whatsoever.

This opposition was consistent with the Church of Scotland's long-standing opposition to gambling. Amongst many pronouncements on the subject, the General Assembly spoke in 1930 'against the use of any method of raising money for Church purposes which involves any semblance of gambling',[18] and in 1972 it affirmed that 'gambling violates Jesus' law of love in principle because of its essential selfishness and increasingly serious consequences.'[19]

However in 1998, after a two year debate, the Church changed its mind. The General Assembly reaffirmed 'their opposition to gambling in all its forms and their particular concerns over the effect of the National Lottery upon the life of the nation',[20] but at the same time authorised 'all agencies of the Church to determine for themselves whether or not to make application for ... Lottery funding', with the proviso that they should first seek alternative sources of finance.[21] Specific areas where Lottery money could be used were defined as 'community work and cultural activities, partnership ventures, work in relation to buildings.'[22]

The Methodist Church initially took a firmer line. At its Conference in 1995 it voted by an overwhelming majority not to seek Lottery funding for the maintenance of church buildings or for personnel employed by the Church. However it also agreed that,

> 'in exceptional circumstances a Methodist project, dedicated to work alongside the poor, might apply to the Charities Board for funds.'[23]

But in 1999 this position was overturned, when the Conference voted 'to permit Church Councils to apply for National Lottery funding for any purpose, at their own discretion.'[24]

In the first four years of its existence the Heritage Lottery Fund made grants worth over £62 million to almost 500 churches of different denominations. Recipients have included the Roman Catholic Church, the Church of England, the Church of Ireland, the Church in Wales, the Scottish Episcopal Church, the Church of Scotland and the United Reformed Church.

The willingness to accept lottery money has disastrous implications for the Church as a whole. It shows the world that biblical teaching can be set at nought when expedient, and that Christians are not willing to pay for their own cause. Thus our lack of trust in God is openly demonstrated. It also lays us open to the charge of hypocrisy, for if it is wrong to gamble, it is equally wrong to accept money from gambling.

On a personal level, there is no doubt that the consciences of some church leaders have been seared. Many have accepted lottery funds, whilst openly expressing doubts and unhappiness about so doing. Thus the leadership of the Church is undermined. Such is the way of Laodicea.

References

1. Gott. K., *The Sunderland Refreshing*, Hodder and Stoughton, 1995, pp. 78, 79. Reproduced by permission of Hodder and Stoughton Ltd.
2. *The Times* 11.3.1998.
3. Earl Ferrers, House of Lords 27.5.1993. *The Parliamentary Debates (Hansard) 5th Series* vol. DXLVI, p. 400. Parliamentary copyright material from Hansard is reproduced with the permission of the Controller of Her Majesty's Stationery Office on behalf of Parliament.
4. *ibid.* p. 413.
5. *ibid.* p. 414.
6. *ibid.* p. 414.
7. *ibid.* p. 415.
8. *ibid.* p. 415.
9. *The Church of England Yearbook*, 1952, Church Assembly, SPCK, p. 173. Extracts from 'The Church of England Yearbook, 1952' are copyright © The Central Board of Finance of the Church of England (1952); The Archbishops' Council, 1999 and are reproduced by permission.
10. *ibid.* p. 173.
11. Earl Ferrers, *Hansard*, p. 401.
12. *Church Times* 16.6.1995.
13. *The National Lottery – Statement by the House of Bishops* 13.1.1995. Extracts from 'The National Lottery – Statement by the House of Bishops' are copyright © The Central Board of Finance of the Church of England, 1995; The Archbishops' Council, 1999 and are reproduced by permission.
14. *ibid.*
15. *ibid.*
16. *ibid.*
17. *The Church of Scotland, Gambling, Raffling and Lotteries*, 1998, p. 8.

18. *ibid.* p. 1.
19. *ibid.* p. 7.
20. *Church of Scotland, A Special Commission anent the National Lottery,* May 1998, p. 33/1.
21. *ibid.* p. 33/1.
22. *ibid.* p. 33/1.
23. *The Methodist Church,* Press Release, 30.6.1995.
24. *The Methodist Conference,* Press Release, 1.7.1999.

MINISTRY

Chapter 18

A Godly Ministry

'I will set shepherds over them who will care for them,
and they shall fear no more, nor be dismayed,
neither shall any be missing, says the LORD.'
(Jeremiah 23:4)

I

A zealous, God-fearing ministry is essential to the life of the Church, for the flock of Christ needs shepherds who will guard it and feed it. A lax and lazy ministry spells disaster, for then the sheep are neither fed, watered, nor sustained in the life of Christ.

The task of the Old Testament priests was to pray, to offer sacrifices, and to teach the law of God.

> *'For the lips of a priest should guard knowledge, and men should seek instruction from his mouth, for he is the messenger of the LORD of hosts.'*   (Malachi 2:7)

In the Old Testament there were many conscientious priests such as Aaron and Ezra. Others, sadly, were not so good. The book of Malachi speaks of priests, who *'have turned aside from the way'* and *'caused many to stumble'* (Malachi 2:8).

Amongst other things, these priests were sacrificing imperfect animals in a perfunctory manner (1:6–9, 13). They were also conniving with laxity in marriage (2:10–16) and in tithing (3:6–12).

After Pentecost, under the Lord's guidance, the Church developed a two-tier ministry. One tier, which we may call universal, looked after the Church as a whole. It consisted of the apostles and their helpers, and was a peripatetic ministry, with the apostles moving from place to place, either founding or strengthening the churches.

The other tier was local. The church in each town or city had a group of leaders, known as elders. These were appointed by apostles, or apostolic delegates. Paul and Barnabas, for example, appointed elders in each of the churches they founded (Acts 14:23). In later years Paul wrote to Titus, instructing him to *'appoint elders in every town as I directed you'* (Titus 1:5).

Alongside the elders was a group of deacons. Whereas the elders were responsible for the spiritual growth of the church, the deacons coped with temporal matters. The first deacons, for example, had the task of organising food relief for Christian widows (Acts 6:1–6).

The work of the ministry, both universal and local, was *'to care for the church of God'* (Acts 20:28), and to this end the Lord gave various gifts, or spiritual endowments.

> *'And His gifts were that some should be apostles, some prophets, some evangelists, some pastors and teachers.'*
>
> (Ephesians 4:11)

These were to be used

> *'to equip the saints for the work of ministry, for building up the body of Christ, until we all attain to the unity of the faith and of the knowledge of the Son of God, to mature manhood, to the measure of the stature of the fullness of Christ.'*
>
> (Ephesians 4:12, 13)

II

As well as describing the shape and the purpose of the Christian ministry, the New Testament gives qualifications for elders and deacons. These are mainly found in Paul's letters to Timothy and Titus.

When writing to Titus, his fellow worker, Paul said,

> *'This is why I left you in Crete, that you might amend what was defective, and appoint elders in every town as I directed you, if any man is blameless, the husband of one wife, and his children are believers and not open to the charge of being profligate or insubordinate. For a bishop, as God's steward, must be blameless; he must not be arrogant or quick-tempered or a drunkard or violent or greedy for gain, but hospitable, a lover of goodness, master of himself, upright, holy, and self-controlled; he must hold firm to the sure word as taught, so that he may be able to give instruction in sound doctrine and also to confute those who contradict it.'* (Titus 1:5–9)

In this passage Paul mentions elders and bishops. These are one and the same. The word 'bishop' means 'overseer', and as such describes the work of the elder in overseeing the church.

Thus when Paul instructed Timothy about the qualities required of a bishop, he was talking about the elders of the church.

> *'Now a bishop must be above reproach, the husband of one wife, temperate, sensible, dignified, hospitable, an apt teacher, no drunkard, not violent but gentle, not quarrelsome, and no lover of money. He must manage his own household well, keeping his children submissive and respectful in every way; for if a man does not know how to manage his own household, how can he care for God's church? He must not be a recent convert, or he may be puffed up with conceit and*

fall into the condemnation of the devil; moreover he must be well thought of by outsiders, or he may fall into reproach and the snare of the devil.' (1 Timothy 3:2–7)

Similar attributes applied to the deacons.

'Deacons likewise must be serious, not double-tongued, nor addicted to much wine, not greedy for gain; they must hold the mystery of the faith with a clear conscience … Let deacons be the husband of one wife, and let them manage their children and their households well.'

(1 Timothy 3:8, 9, 12)

Three of these qualifications are under special attack at this time.

The first is that both elders and deacons must truly believe the faith. The elder *'must hold firm to the sure word as taught'* (Titus 1:9), and the deacon *'must hold the mystery of the faith with a clear conscience'* (1 Timothy 3:9). This is so that the church leader is able *'to give instruction in sound doctrine and also to confute those who contradict it'* (Titus 1:9).

Secondly, the leadership of the church should be male. Both the elder and the deacon are to be *'the husband of one wife'* (1 Timothy 3:2, 12; Titus 1:6). Throughout these passages Paul describes both the elders and deacons as *'he'*, and *'a man'*.

Thirdly, the leader must set a good example of Christian living. He must not, for example, be *'arrogant or quick-tempered'* (Titus 1:7). Neither should he be a drunkard (1 Timothy 3:3), or *'greedy for gain'* (1 Timothy 3:8). Rather he must be *'temperate, sensible, dignified, hospitable'* (1 Timothy 3:2), *'upright, holy and self-controlled'* (Titus 1:8). His home life should be exemplary, with a stable marriage and well-behaved children (1 Timothy 3:2, 4). As *'the husband of one wife'* (1 Timothy 3:2, 12; Titus 1:6) the leader should neither be polygamous, nor divorced and remarried.

It could be said that the standards set in these passages are impossible to fulfil, and should therefore be treated lightly, or even ignored. Yet these are God's requirements for the ministry of His Church. They are not man-made rules that applied only to the early Christian era. As God calls weak and sinful men to His ministry, we can be sure that He will equip them for the task. All that is required of those called is a willingness, by God's grace, to conform to His criteria.

Chapter 19

A Believing Ministry

'We too believe, and so we speak.'
(2 Corinthians 4:13b)

I

The early Christians had to cope with the problem of false teachers and leaders. This was something they had been warned about, for in the days before His death Jesus told His apostles,

> *'False Christs and false prophets will arise and show signs and wonders, to lead astray, if possible, the elect.'*
>
> (Mark 13:22)

It was not long before such men made their presence felt. We have already seen that the church in Colossae was in danger of being perverted by false teachers,[1] and other churches had similar problems. Paul warned the Galatian Christians that *'there are some who trouble you and want to pervert the gospel of Christ'* (Galatians 1:7). He appealed to the Roman Christians *'to take note of those who create dissensions and difficulties, in opposition to the doctrine which you have been taught'* (Romans 16:17). The Corinthian church was disturbed by *'false apostles, deceitful workmen, disguising themselves as apostles of Christ'* (2 Corinthians 11:13).

Some false teachers actually wrote letters in the name of Paul in order to get their message accepted. Thus we find Paul telling the Thessalonians,

> *'not to be quickly shaken in mind or excited, either by spirit or by word, or by letter purporting to be from us, to the effect that the day of the Lord has come.'*   (2 Thessalonians 2:2)

The apostle John warned his readers that *'many antichrists have come'* (1 John 2:18), who deny the Father and the Son (1 John 2:22). He also told the *'elect lady and her children'* (2 John 1) that,

> *'many deceivers have gone out into the world, men who will not acknowledge the coming of Jesus Christ in the flesh; such a one is the deceiver and the antichrist.'*   (2 John 7)

The apostles were aware that false teachers and leaders would continue to trouble the Church in the future. Peter, in his old age, forewarned his readers that,

> *'there will be false teachers among you, who will secretly bring in destructive heresies, even denying the Master who bought them.'*   (2 Peter 2:1)

Paul told the Ephesian elders,

> *'I know that after my departure fierce wolves will come in among you, not sparing the flock; and from among your own selves will arise men speaking perverse things, to draw away the disciples after them.'*   (Acts 20:29, 30)

In fact the early Church leaders knew that false teachers would always plague the Church. Peter foretold that men who mocked the second coming of the Lord would appear *'in the last days'* (2 Peter 3:3).

The question, therefore, was not whether there would be false teachers and leaders, but what should be done about them. The answer was tough and uncompromising. False teachers had first to be charged *'not to teach any different doctrine'* (1 Timothy 1:3). If, however, they persisted in their errors, the rest of the church must have nothing to do with them. Paul told the Roman Christians to *'avoid'* those who created dissensions (Romans 16:17), and instructed Timothy to *'avoid ... those who make their way into households and capture weak women'* (2 Timothy 3:5, 6). John instructed the elect lady that if any one comes who *'does not abide in the doctrine of Christ'* (2 John 9),

> *'do not receive him into the house or give him any greeting; for he who greets him shares his wicked work.'*
>
> (2 John 10, 11)

The apostles were vigorous and forthright in their opposition to false teachers. Paul pulled no punches when warning the Colossians about the heretics in their midst, and was quite open in his desire *'to undermine the claim'* of the false apostles in Corinth (2 Corinthians 11:12). Paul's strongest comments came in his letter to the Galatians, where he said,

> *'If any one is preaching to you a gospel contrary to that which you received, let him be accursed.'*   (Galatians 1:9)

The false teachers in Galatia were trying to impose circumcision on the Gentile Christians, and Paul went so far as to say,

> *'I wish those who unsettle you would mutilate themselves.'*
>
> (Galatians 5:12)

The reason for such strong language was a deep love for the Church. Wrong teaching led people away from the truth, and put their eternal salvation in jeopardy. Paul told the Galatians that those who accept the doctrine of the false teachers are *'severed from Christ'* (Galatians 5:4), and have believed in vain. Some years later John warned Christians about false teachers so that *'you may not lose what you have worked for, but may win a full reward'* (2 John 8).

II

The merest glance at the subsequent history of the Church shows the accuracy of the apostle's predictions. False teachers and leaders have appeared down the ages, and led many astray.

To its credit the Church tried to follow the biblical instructions and protect its members from unbelieving leaders. Sadly it went too far on many occasions, and dealt with false teachers by the worldly methods of sword and fire. At times it became paranoic and instituted inquisitions and witch hunts, and in times when the Church itself was corrupt it tried to crush those who genuinely desired godly reformation.

Nevertheless, despite all these aberrations, the biblical injunctions still stand. False teachers and leaders must not be accepted. Every attempt must be made to help them to see the truth and correct their teaching. If this approach fails such teachers are to be avoided, because they lead the flock away from eternal salvation.

III

It is a matter of extreme concern that in our days false teachers are not avoided. Rather they are accepted and even given high office in the Church.

One of the marks of our western liberal world is toleration in matters of religion. Until the latter years of the 17th century, governments sought to impose just one version of Christianity on their subjects, with penalties laid upon those who followed other ways. Thus Protestants were persecuted in Roman Catholic countries, and Catholics in Protestant lands.

This policy led to civil unrest and religious wars, which exhausted the European nations and produced a disillusionment with the whole idea of uniformity. Governments began to tolerate other Christian churches in their midst, and this resulted in a removal of the legal penalties and civil disabilities on nonconformists. In due course toleration extended to believers of other faiths.

Sadly the spirit of toleration began to affect Christian doctrine. Various writers, thinkers and leaders propounded opinions contrary to the Christian faith, and yet claimed the liberty to remain within the Church and even teach therein. A survey of Church history over the last two hundred years or more shows a gradual acceptance of such heretical teaching. The Church followed the world in a thoroughly Laodicean spirit.

IV

The consecration of Dr David Jenkins as Bishop of Durham in July 1984 was a defining moment in this process.

During a television interview some weeks before his consecration Dr Jenkins denied, or cast doubt upon, a number of fundamental Christian beliefs. These included the virginal conception of Jesus, His bodily resurrection and His divinity. Regarding the virgin birth, Dr Jenkins said,

> 'The virgin birth, I'm pretty clear, is a story told after the event in order to express and symbolise a faith that this Jesus was a unique event from God.'[2]

He then said the birth stories of Jesus were legends,[3] and not historical records.[4]

Dr Jenkins also denied the physical resurrection of Jesus. Whilst claiming to believe in the resurrection, he said,

> 'I hold the view that he rose from the dead. The question is what that means, isn't it? . . .

> ... I don't think the resurrection is "a miracle" – that
> is to say, that it doesn't seem to me reading the records
> as they remain in both the gospels and what Paul says
> (in) 1 Corinthians, that there was any one event which
> you could identify with the resurrection.'[5]

In place of an empty tomb, Dr Jenkins postulated 'a series
of experiences' which,

> 'gradually convinced a growing number of people who
> became apostles that Jesus had certainly been dead,
> certainly buried and he wasn't finished, and what is
> more he wasn't just not finished but he was raised up.'[6]

By 'raised up' Dr Jenkins meant,

> 'the very life and power and purpose and personality
> which was in him was actually continuing and was
> continuing both in the sphere of God and in the sphere
> of history so that he was a risen and living presence and
> possibility.'[7]

In an interview after his consecration, the bishop remarked
that,

> 'to believe in a Christian way you don't have to neces-
> sarily have a precise belief that the risen Jesus had a
> literally physical body.'[8]

He further described the bodily resurrection of Jesus as 'a
conjuring trick with bones',[9] and in an earlier interview
suggested that the physical body of Jesus had been left in
the tomb, or removed by the disciples.[10]

Dr Jenkins also held it permissible for someone to disbelieve the divinity of Jesus, and yet be a Christian. In his
original television interview, he was asked,

'If (a man) says, I believe passionately in Jesus as a great moral teacher and a divine agent and he's leading me towards God, but I don't believe that he was God-made-flesh, is he still a Christian?' [11]

His reply was simply, 'Oh, yes, yes.' [12] He did not say that he himself doubted the divinity of Jesus, but that the belief was not essential.

It is obvious that the bishop-elect's views were at total variance with the teachings of the Bible and the traditional beliefs of the Church. The Scriptures teach unequivocally that the virginal conception of Jesus was a historical fact, that the tomb was empty on Easter Day, and that our Lord is truly human and truly divine. It is not surprising, therefore, to find that Dr Jenkin's view of the Bible was that,

'There's absolutely no certainty in the New Testament about anything of importance.' [13]

Such opinions were not novel. Many people in the Church at large, both lay and ordained, had long taken such positions. In fact many regarded Dr Jenkins as an old-fashioned liberal, whose ideas were shaped by a late 19th century world view. The main difference in this case was that Dr Jenkins not only held views contrary to the Christian faith, but he was willing to pronounce them openly and even propagate them.

However, despite knowing his views, the Church authorities proceeded with Dr Jenkin's consecration. Over thirty bishops took part in the ceremony, and laid their hands upon the new bishop of Durham. Although not every bishop agreed with Dr Jenkin's beliefs, they all partook in his consecration.

A watershed had been reached, for it had been publicly proclaimed that a man who denied the most basic and glorious truths of our faith was fit to be a bishop. The biblical injunctions concerning Church leaders had been overturned, and a spirit of worldly toleration was triumphant. The barriers were down, and further unbelief could be openly proclaimed by Christian leaders.

V

As a result of the Durham controversy the Church of England bishops produced a report entitled *The Nature of Christian Belief*. This showed for the first time that heretical opinions were held and accepted without criticism. Although the report was written in carefully chosen words, it was clear that the bishops disagreed amongst themselves on the question of the historicity of the virginal conception and the empty tomb.

The bishops wrote,

> 'The divergences between Christian scholars on the relation of the Virginal Conception of our Lord to this great mystery (that is, the Incarnation), and on the question whether or not that Conception is to be regarded as historical fact as well as imagery symbolic of divine truth, have been indicated, and they are reflected in the convictions of members of this House.' [14]

Of the resurrection they said,

> 'On the question whether ... Christ's tomb that first Easter Day was empty we recognise that scholarship can offer no conclusive demonstration; and the divergent views to be found among scholars of standing are reflected in the thinking of individual bishops.' [15]

These remarks also showed that scholars who deviated from the Scriptures were accepted as teachers in the Church. This inevitably leads to doctrinal confusion.

During the 1990s things went from bad to worse, with many leaders teaching unbiblical doctrines, whilst retaining their good standing in the Church.

Perhaps the most radical statement of recent times has come from the Rt Rev. John Spong, the then Bishop of Newark in the Episcopal Church of the United States. In 1998 he posted twelve theses on his church's Internet site, and called upon Christians to debate them. The theses are as follows,

'1. Theism, as a way of defining God is dead. So most theological God-talk is today meaningless. A new way to speak of God must be found.

2. Since God can no longer be conceived in theistic terms, it becomes nonsensical to seek to understand Jesus as the incarnation of the theistic deity. So the christology of the age is bankrupt.

3. The biblical story of the perfect and finished creation from which human beings fell into sin is pre-Darwinian mythology and post-Darwinian nonsense.

4. The virgin birth, understood as literal biology, makes Christ's divinity, as traditionally understood, impossible.

5. The miracle stories of the New Testament can no longer be interpreted in a post-Newtonian world as supernatural events performed by an incarnate deity.

6. The view of the cross as the sacrifice for the sins of the world is a barbarian idea based on primitive concepts of God, and must be dismissed.

7. Resurrection is an action of God. Jesus was raised into the meaning of God. It therefore cannot be a physical resuscitation occurring inside human history.

8. The story of the Ascension assumed a three-tiered universe and is therefore not capable of being translated into the concepts of a post-Copernican space age.

9. There is no external, objective, revealed standard writ in scripture or on tablets of stone that will govern our ethical behaviour for all time.

10. Prayer cannot be a request made to a theistic deity to act in human history in a particular way.

11. The hope for life after death must be separated for ever from the behaviour-control mentality of reward and punishment. The Church must abandon, therefore, its reliance on guilt as a motivator for behaviour.

12. All human beings bear God's image and must be respected for what each person is. Therefore, no external description of one's being, whether based on race, ethnicity, gender or sexual orientation, can properly be used as the basis for either rejection or discrimination.' [16]

It is patently obvious that Dr Spong drove a coach and horses through biblical and traditional Christian belief. All the major beliefs of the Church were discarded on the basis of modern science and philosophy. Yet he continued to work as a bishop in the Church until his retirement. Despite protests from some clergy of the Church of England, he was welcomed at the 1998 Lambeth Conference. His opinions did not put him outside the Anglican pale. Thus the conclusion can be drawn that such views, although diametrically opposed to the true faith, are acceptable within modern-day Anglicanism.

It is impossible to estimate how many church leaders agree with Bishops Jenkins and Spong. Obviously some do. Others who do not are prepared to show a spirit of toleration, and accept them as Christian leaders. The Body of Christ as a whole is sliding into the morass of Laodicean compromise. Secular toleration has overturned biblical injunction, with each man believing what is right in his own eyes. No consistent teaching is given by the leadership. The Church is confused, and evangelistically disabled.

References

1. See chapter 3 p. 17.
2. *Credo*, London Weekend Television, 29.4.1984, transcript p. 9.

3. *ibid.* p. 9.
4. *ibid.* p. 10.
5. *ibid.* p. 10.
6. *ibid.* p. 10.
7. *ibid.* p. 10.
8. *Poles Apart*, Radio 4, 28.10.1984. Quoted in W. Ledwich, *The Durham Affair*, Stylite Publishing Ltd, 1985, p. 50.
9. *ibid.* p. 50.
10. *Nightline*, LBC 18.7.1984. Quoted in W. Ledwich, *The Durham Affair*, p. 50. The original transcript is no longer available.
11. *Credo* p. 15.
12. *ibid.* p. 15.
13. Interview on Radio 4, 27.5.1984.
14. *The Nature of Christian Belief*, Church House Publishing, 1986, p. 32. Extracts from 'The Nature of Christian Belief' are copyright © The Central Board of Finance of the Church of England, 1986; The Archbishops' Council, 1999 and are reproduced by permission.
15. *ibid.* p. 25.
16. *Church Times* 17.7.1998.

Chapter 20

A Male Leadership

'A bishop must be ... the husband of one wife.'
(1 Timothy 3:2)

'Let deacons be the husband of one wife.'
(1 Timothy 3:12)

I

There has been a growing movement throughout the 20th century to open the leadership of the Church to women.

In Britain the free churches have been in the forefront of this trend. Amongst others the Methodist Church, the United Reformed Church and the churches in the Baptist Union have women ministers who act on equal terms with men.

The established churches have followed the same path, and the Church of Scotland started ordaining women ministers in 1969. In that same year the Church of England admitted women as lay readers, and in 1975 its General Synod passed a resolution stating,

> 'That this Synod considers that there are no funda-
> mental objections to the ordination of women to the
> priesthood.'

The matter was taken no further at that time because of a significant division of opinion within the dioceses,[1] but in 1987 women were ordained as deacons, and in 1992 the General Synod finally voted to ordain women as priests.

Other Anglican provinces including the United States, New Zealand, Canada, Hong Kong, Uganda, Brazil, Scotland and Ireland had ordained women priests before 1992, and others, such as Australia, South Africa and Wales, have done so since. Some provinces have gone a step further and consecrated women bishops. In 1989 the Episcopal Church of the United States consecrated the first woman bishop. The Anglican Church in New Zealand took a similar step two years later. By 1998 the number of women bishops had grown to eleven, one in New Zealand, two in Canada, and eight in the United States.

In Europe the Danish Lutheran Church ordained its first woman priest in 1948, and the Norwegian and Swedish Lutherans followed suit in the early 1960s. Both the Norwegian and Swedish Churches consecrated women bishops in the mid-1990s. The German Old Catholic Church, which like all European Old Catholic churches is in full communion with the Church of England, ordained women priests in 1996. The Austrian Old Catholics took the same step in 1998.

However the Orthodox and Roman Catholic churches have resisted opening the priesthood to women. The Orthodox claim it is not on their agenda, and the Pope has stated that it is impossible for a woman to be ordained as a priest. Nevertheless there is a considerable body of opinion within the Roman church which is in favour of the move.

Not all Church members agree with the concept of women clergy, and various arrangements have been made to encourage dissenters to remain within the fold. The Church of England, for example, officially recognises 'two integrities' within the Church, and appointed so-called flying bishops to care for the objectors. In Norway male pastors are not compelled to celebrate the Eucharist with female colleagues, and pastoral oversight by the cathedral dean has been offered to dissenters in the diocese of Hamar, where the bishop is a woman. Despite these safeguards, some Church members have joined other Christian bodies whilst others have dropped out altogether.

In a few churches, such as the Lutheran church in Sweden, and the Anglican churches in the United States and Canada, concessions to the traditionalists have been slowly withdrawn. The Episcopal Church in the USA, for example, mandated commitment to the ordination of women at its General Convention in 1997. This means that 'all must accept it in practice and every diocese shall ordain women', and those who oppose women priests 'must be excluded from being bishops, priests and deacons, and from serving in lay leadership positions.'[2] Three years later three diocese had still not ordained women, and in July 2000 the ECUSA General Convention voted to send a task force to compel compliance with church policy.[3]

On the other hand two churches, the Presbyterian Church of Australia and the Polish Mariavite Church have actually abandoned the ordination of women.

II

Women leaders are not found in the Bible nor in the tradition of the Church. We have already noted the scriptural teaching that the responsibility of Church leadership devolves on men.[4] This is nothing to do with supposed male superiority, neither does it deny that women have a ministry in the Church. We read throughout the New Testament of women ministering in various ways. Such include Anna the prophetess (Luke 2:36–38), Mary Magdalene, Joanna and Susanna (Luke 8:2, 3); Tabitha (Acts 9:36–43), Priscilla (Acts 18:1–4, 26), Phoebe (Romans 16:1) and above all the Virgin Mary who had the unique task of being the mother of our Lord. Nevertheless these holy women did not lead the Church.

Consonant with the teaching of male leadership in the second chapter of Genesis,[5] all priests in Israel were male.

Unlike nations around them, the Jews had no female priests. There were women prophetesses such as Miriam, the sister of Moses (Exodus 15:20), Deborah (Judges 4:5) and Huldah (2 Kings 22:14), but they did not exercise ultimate authority. When the officials of King Josiah went to the prophetess Huldah to inquire of the Lord about the recently found book of the law, they listened to what she had to say, and then reported back to the King. It was the task of Josiah to test, and if need be to act upon, her words (2 Kings 22, 23). He, not Huldah, bore the authority and responsibility of leadership. Similarly Deborah did not act against Sisera by her own authority, but encouraged the leadership of Barak (Judges 4:6ff).

The prophet Isaiah, speaking the words of God, said one mark of a people who had strayed from the Lord was that they would be led by women and children.

'Woe to the wicked! It shall be ill with him,
for what his hands have done shall be done to him.
My people – children are their oppressors,
  and women rule over them.
O my people, your leaders mislead you,
  and confuse the course of your paths.'   (Isaiah 3:11, 12)

The truth of male leadership is shown in Jesus' choice of the twelve apostles. Before He chose the twelve Jesus spent the whole night in prayer, seeking His Father's mind. Many people followed Jesus at that time, so the twelve were not automatic appointees.

'In these days He went out to the mountain to pray; and all
night He continued in prayer to God.'   (Luke 6:12)

Jesus' prayers were answered for,

'when it was day, He called His disciples, and chose from
them twelve, whom He named apostles.'   (Luke 6:13)

Even though many women followed Him and ministered to His needs, the chosen twelve were men.

It is important to realise that the twelve were the choice of God the Father. This is why Mark could say that Jesus, *'called to Him those whom He desired'* (Mark 3:13). He desired these men because they were those whom His Father willed. Jesus was not being constrained by social conventions, but was obeying His Father.

Some three years later, when the Church sought to fill the vacancy in the apostleship arising from the death of Judas, Peter said,

> *'One of the men who have accompanied us during all the time that the Lord Jesus went in and out among us, beginning from the baptism of John until the day when He was taken up from us – one of these men must become with us a witness to His resurrection.'*   (Acts 1:21–22)

Peter specifically said *'men'*. The new apostle had to be a man, because this was where leadership properly belonged. Peter, like Paul in later years, was following the precepts of His Lord.

It is within this context of male leadership that some instructions of Paul, which sound harsh to modern ears, make sense. He said to the Corinthians,

> *'As in all the churches of the saints, the women should keep silence in the churches. For they are not permitted to speak, but should be subordinate, as even the law says. If there is anything they desire to know, let them ask their husbands at home. For it is shameful for a woman to speak in church.'*
>   (1 Corinthians 14:33–35)

He also told Timothy,

> *'Let a woman learn in silence with all submissiveness. I permit no woman to teach or to have authority over men; she is to keep silent. For Adam was formed first, then Eve; and*

Adam was not deceived, but the woman was deceived and became a transgressor.' (1 Timothy 2:11–14)

On both occasions Paul refers back to the Old Testament to justify his teaching. He knew well that Jesus had not come to overthrow the law, but to fulfil it.

There is throughout the Bible a strong concept of authority and headship, with both male and female under subjection. Paul summed it up in his first letter to the Corinthians, where he wrote,

'I want you to understand that the head of every man is Christ, the head of a woman is her husband, and the head of Christ is God.' (1 Corinthians 11:3)

This verse speaks of God's wise ordering of His creation, and also of the sacrifice involved in leadership. The headship of Christ was shown in love and sacrifice, culminating in the Cross. Such a headship is to be reflected in the relationship of men and women, both in marriage (Ephesians 5) and in leading the Church. Man is the head of woman in self-giving love, which involves total sacrifice on his part. All is organised in this way by God for our good, that we may *'grow up in every way into Him who is the head, into Christ'* (Ephesians 4:15). We rebel against it at our peril.

III

The proponents of women's ordination have majored on one verse of Scripture,

'There is neither Jew nor Greek, there is neither slave nor free, there is neither male nor female; for you are all one in Christ Jesus.' (Galatians 3:28)

This was often quoted as the decisive and final word on the whole subject, and was used as the scriptural motto of the Movement for the Ordination of Women.

The thrust of this verse is that whatever our race, social position or sex, we are all saved through faith in Christ. Once we have put our faith in Him, we are freely justified, accepted as sons of God, and able to receive all the benefits of that relationship. It is faith alone which brings salvation, and the way is open to all.

Galatians 3:28 has nothing to do with the ordination of women, or the headship of women within the Church. Paul is talking about our salvation, not our work within the Church. There is no mention in Galatians of the place and relationship of men and women within the life and organisation of the Church. Paul is, at it were, showing us the way into the Church, but not speaking about what happens once inside.

Thus there is no contradiction between *'there is neither male nor female; for you are all one in Christ Jesus'* and *'I permit no woman to teach or to have authority over men.'* The first speaks of our status before God, and the second of our function in the Church. Being saved does not make a man any less a man, nor a woman any less a woman. Rather it enhances our masculinity or femininity.

It is also held by those in favour of women priests that various women had positions of leadership in the early Church. Four names, Priscilla, Phoebe, Junias and Mary Magdalene have been singled out. We will consider each in turn.

Priscilla and her husband Aquila are mentioned six times in the New Testament. In Acts 18 we read of them helping Apollos, an enthusiastic and powerful Christian preacher, who *'had been instructed in the way of the Lord ... though he knew only the baptism of John'* (Acts 18:25). After he had spoken in the synagogue at Ephesus, Priscilla and Aquila *'took him and expounded to him the way of God more accurately'* (Acts 18:26).

It is claimed that here is 'important evidence for the fact that women did, on occasion, teach men.'[6] From that position it is easy to take things a step further and see Priscilla as a teacher in the Church. However, this verse merely tells of a Christian couple quietly taking a keen and dedicated, but raw Christian, to one side and putting him right about certain matters of belief.

Great play is also made of the fact that Priscilla's name is sometimes mentioned before that of Aquila.

> 'Priscilla is named before her husband in four out of the six references to her, which is about as odd as speaking of Mrs and Mr Smith would be today. The best explanation seems to be that she was "the more active Christian" or "more capable than her husband." ' [7]

Such a conclusion is highly debatable. Even if Priscilla had been mentioned first in all six references, it would hardly constitute a basis for saying women had positions of leadership in the early Church. In fact the order of the names means nothing. While we would not normally say Mrs and Mr Smith, we do say 'mum and dad' or 'grandma and grandad', and either 'father and mother' or 'mother and father', without any indication as to who is the head of the house. Similarly when referring to couples by their first names we sometimes put the man's name first and sometimes the woman's. It can depend on whom we knew first, or the rhythm and flow of the two names.

Phoebe is mentioned in Romans where Paul wrote,

> *'I commend to you our sister Phoebe, a deaconess of the church at Cenchreae, that you may receive her in the Lord as befits the saints, and help her in whatever she may require from you, for she has been a helper of many and of myself as well.'*   (Romans 16:1, 2)

Although Phoebe is described in our translation as a deaconess, the actual word used is the masculine 'deacon'. This is the same word Paul employed in 1 Timothy 3:8. Hence it is alleged that Phoebe held that office and was therefore in a position of leadership.

However, the matter is not so straightforward, for in 1 Timothy, Paul insists that deacons are to be the husband of one wife. Thus on that ground Phoebe could not have held the office of deacon.

Some translations of the Bible, such as the Authorised Version, the Revised Version, and the New King James Version, have recognised this difficulty. They have described Phoebe as a 'servant', which is a correct translation of the word 'deacon'. This, of course, in no way belittles the blessings she obviously brought to many through her ministrations.

Junias appears in the same chapter of Romans.

> *'Greet Andronicus and Junias, my kinsmen and my fellow prisoners; they are men of note among the apostles, and they were in Christ before me.'* (Romans 16:7)

It is claimed that Junias was a woman, and that she and Andronicus, presumably her husband, were apostles.[8] This is not a new thought, but it is impossible to tell from the Greek whether Junias is male or female. The words *'men of note'* do not help, because *'men'* does not appear in the original text. A better translation is the Authorised Version's, *'who are of note among the apostles'*. Further it is not clear whether Andronicus and Junias were in fact apostles, or whether 'from their active co-operation with the Apostles, were well known to them and distinguished among them.'[9]

Mary Magdalene has also been seen as an apostle, based on her meeting the risen Jesus on Easter morning. There Jesus said to her,

> *'Do not hold me, for I have not yet ascended to the Father; but go to my brethren and say to them, I am ascending to my Father and your Father, to my God and your God.'* (John 20:17)

The noun 'apostle' comes from a Greek verb which means 'to send', and because Mary was sent by Jesus with a message to the disciples, some have called her the apostle to the apostles,[10] or the first apostle. Yet we do not call someone an apostle simply because Jesus gave them a message to deliver. Jesus told the Gadarene ex-demoniac to,

> *'Go home to your friends, and tell them how much the Lord has done for you, and how He has had mercy on you.'*
>
> (Mark 5:19).

Nobody would dream of calling this man an apostle, and neither can we call Mary Magdalene an apostle. The fact that she had to deliver a message from the Lord does not make her a leader in the Church.

Although these examples show that women were greatly used in a variety of ways in the apostolic Church, none of them show that women were in positions of leadership. The biblical teaching is clear and unambiguous, and until recently the Church as a whole has been faithful to the Word of God.

IV

Ruth B. Edwards has given two reasons for the rise of women clergy. One is 'the revolution that has taken place in theological thinking, occasioned partly by the modern critical approach to biblical study and partly by a new readiness to recognize that the Holy Spirit operates in people's lives without restriction to official church channels.'[11] This, she claims, makes it no longer possible 'for any denomination to look back to the New Testament and claim quite simply that here is the source and pattern of its ministry'.[12]

The other reason is the 'changing social attitudes and roles' of men and women. Women are now educated 'similarly, if not identically, to men', having 'their legal and political equality officially recognised', and 'the vast majority of professions open to them.' They also have 'potential freedom from domestic drudgery and the continual round of child bearing'.[13]

In other words, female leadership in the Church is a product of the age. It is our liberal society, and that alone, which has gestated and given birth to women leaders in the Church.

The Church, as David Pawson says, 'is trailing the world in opening the ranks of leadership to women.' [14]

The power of present-day social attitudes was well expressed in 1988 by the then Archbishop of York, who in a personal credo said,

> 'I believe women ought to be ordained to the priesthood. I believe it is for the fundamental reason summed up in the idea of Christ's inclusive humanity. I believe that truths which were there from the beginning in the Christian faith can lie dormant until the social and psychological conditions are right for them to be perceived. And I affirm that the time has come to express this truth in the life of the church, and that is not going to go away.' [15]

The concept that Christian truths can lie dormant and unseen until human social conditions and knowledge bring them out into the open has always been the cry of liberalism. It springs from a stance which gives greater authority to the culture of the day than to the abiding Word of God.

This does not deny the great good that has resulted from movements for women's rights. Over the centuries women have been crushed and exploited by men, and many still are. Although much has still to be accomplished women are more and more treated as people in their own right.

However, it is quite wrong to take our modern suppositions and ideas, and transfer them directly to the abiding truths of the Christian faith. As Christians we have something deeper and far more satisfying than anything the world can give. In Christ both men and women are accepted by God through faith, and fulfilled within the roles created for them by their loving Father.

References

1. *The Ordination of Women to the Priesthood. A Second Report by the House of Bishops of the General Synod of the Church of England*, 1988, pp. 3, 4.
2. P. Toon, *Are Modern Liberal Episcopalians Truly Liberal?* Faith and Heritage, Spring 1998, p. 15.
3. *Church Times* 21.7.00.
4. Chapter 18 p. 151.
5. Chapter 12 p. 83.
6. Ruth B. Edwards, *The Case for Women's Ministry*, p. 57.
7. *ibid.* pp. 57, 58.
8. *ibid.* p. 58.
9. R. Haldane, *The Epistle to the Romans*, Banner of Truth, 1958, p. 637.
10. Ruth B. Edwards, *The Case for Women's Ministry*, p. 46.
11. *ibid.* p. 11.
12. *ibid.* p. 12.
13. *ibid.* p. 2.
14. J. David Pawson, *Leadership is Male*, Highland Books, 1989, p. 12.
15. J. Habgood, 'Sermon in York Minster', quoted in the leaflet, *The Time is now – Join us now*, Movement for the Ordination of Women.

Chapter 21

A Moral Ministry

'A bishop, as God's steward, must be blameless ...
upright, holy, and self-controlled.'
(Titus 1:7, 8)

'Deacons, likewise, must be serious, not double-tongued,
not addicted to much wine, not greedy for gain.'
(1 Timothy 3:8)

I

A high standard of Christian living is an absolute essential for the ministry. The minister is in a real sense the representative of God, and is called to reflect the holiness and power of the Lord. As members of the church look to their leader, so they should see something of the nature of God Himself.

If the Church is led by devout and upright men, their example will percolate through the rest of the body, and the members will be encouraged to live godly lives. A Christian leader who lives a sinful life is unable to teach the moral demands of a holy God. If his own house is not in order, he is in no position to lead others in the way of righteousness.

This is why Paul told the elders of the Ephesian church to *'take heed to yourselves'* (Acts 20:28). They had to watch their own lives, so that they were fit to lead the flock of Christ.

Paul also urged the Corinthian Christians to *'be imitators of me'* (1 Corinthians 4:16), and he rejoiced that the Thessalonians *'became imitators of us and of the Lord'* (1 Thessalonians 1:6).

Christian leaders are especially open to temptation, for if the shepherd is smitten, then the sheep are scattered. Knowing this, the Church has always been concerned that the personal lives of its clergy should be of the highest order. In the Church of England candidates for ordination were asked,

> 'Will you be diligent to frame and fashion your own selves, and your families, according to the doctrine of Christ; and to make both yourselves and them, as much as in you lieth, wholesome examples and patterns to the flock of Christ?' [1]

In a similar manner the Puritan Richard Baxter exhorted his fellow-ministers,

> 'Take heed to yourselves, lest your example contradict your doctrine ... lest you unsay with your lives, what you say with your tongues.' [2]

Although there have always been bad apples, it is a tribute to the dedication of the ministry down the centuries that these have been the exception rather than the rule.

However in our generation two serious compromises have wormed their way into the life of the ministry. One concerns the marital status of ministers, and the other relates to the ordination of active homosexuals. The way these compromises have developed in the Church of England is common to many branches of the Church.

II

We have already seen that divorce and remarriage are never the will of God, [3] and that the Christian leader must be neither a polygamist, nor divorced and remarried whilst his former partner is alive. [4]

Until recently the Church of England faithfully applied this teaching both to those seeking ordination, and to serving clergymen.

Regarding ordinands Canon C4.3 of the law of the Church said,

> 'No person shall be admitted into holy orders who has remarried and, the wife of that marriage being alive, has a former wife still living; or who is married to a person who has been previously married and whose former husband is still living.' [5]

In 1978 the report *Marriage and the Church's Task*, which we noted in an earlier chapter,[6] stated that,

> 'The increasing number of people who have been divorced is ... leading to a growing number of ordinands and clergymen themselves marrying, or seeking to marry, divorced women.' [7]

Because of this the authors of the report recommended legislation which would,

> 'give the diocesan bishop discretion whether or not to ordain a man who:
> (a) having been divorced has remarried during the lifetime of his former wife; or
> (b) has married a divorced woman during the lifetime of her former husband.' [8]

This legislation appeared in the 1990 Clergy (Ordination) Measure. Canon C4.3 was adjusted accordingly, and the Archbishops of Canterbury and York were empowered to allow the ordination of those whose marital state had previously been an impediment to holy orders.[9] Thus the teaching of the Word of God had been overruled in conformity with the spirit of the age.

A parallel compromise has occurred with regard to serving clergy. The position of a divorced clergyman in the Church of England was always insecure. This was more so if the said clergyman had remarried during the lifetime of his former spouse, or was married to a divorcee whose previous husband was still alive. A bishop could deal with such situations by asking the clergyman to resign from his living, or remove him from his parish, or refuse to institute him to another benefice. However the legal basis for such procedures was unclear, and it was authoritatively stated that,

'The law on the marriage and divorce of ordinands and clergy is confusing and, in some respects doubtful.' [10]

A clergyman was liable to be deprived of his benefice if he was divorced because of his 'adultery, desertion or intolerable conduct,' [11] but if the divorced clergyman was the so-called innocent party it was doubtful whether any discipline could be applied. Should, however, the clergyman remarry during the lifetime of his former spouse 'the position becomes less clear.' [12]

The report *Marriage and the Church's Task* addressed this situation. It recommended legislation to allow the bishop discretion whether or not to institute a clergyman who had been divorced and remarried, whilst his previous wife was still alive, or who had married a divorcee during the lifetime of her ex-husband. [13]

The situation has changed considerably since this report was published. Although no statistics are available so far as the Church of England is concerned, it is known that clergy marriages are collapsing at an increasing rate. In 1991 Roger Hennessey, a social worker in Norwich diocese, reported that, 'during the last decade there has been an increase in the rate of marriage breakdowns among Church of England clergymen which has mirrored the wider social trend towards higher rates of divorce.' [14] He estimated that 'each diocese, on the basis of statistics drawn together by the Bishops, may expect at least one breakdown per year.'[15] The growing problem was acknowledged by the General Synod in 1993 in a motion referring to 'the increasing numbers of clergy marriages suffering breakdown.'[16] According to the charity Corporation of the Sons of the Clergy, a 'noticeable growth area' in 1996 was the 40% increase in grants made 'in cases of (clergy) marital breakdown.'[17] In 1997 a consultation paper *Support for Clergy Marriages*, produced under the chairmanship of the Bishop of Winchester, bemoaned the lack of hard data but regarded the problem of clergy marriage breakdown 'as serious and increasing.'[18] It has been estimated that the number of divorces among clergy has now reached the same level as that of the rest of society.[19] The existence of the organisation Broken Rites, a support group for divorced and separated clergy wives, is eloquent testimony to a real problem.

Similarly there is no data on the number of clergy who remarry after divorce, or who marry divorcees. Yet it is common knowledge that an increasing number of clergy are in this situation, many of whom continue in active ministry, with some promoted to high office.

Some well publicised instances in the 1990s highlight the problem.

In 1995, after his third marriage, the Rev. Kit Chalcraft was asked by his bishop to resign. He had not, however, been asked to go after his second marriage. It was also disclosed, during the ensuing controversy, that there was another priest in the same diocese who was thrice married. This priest had resigned and had worked in secular employment for two years. He had then been given permission to officiate in the diocese.[20] In 1997 the Bishop of Birmingham married a divorcee whose first husband was alive, and who worked as a non-stipendiary priest in the same diocese.[21] The bishop continued to officiate.

The Church of England is far from the only Church involved in this compromise. About one third of the clergy of the Episcopal Church in the United States are both divorced and remarried, and some are in serial marriages.[22]

III

The ordination of practising homosexual clergy is an area of passionate debate within the Church at the present time.

Tremendous pressure has been exerted on the Church of England in recent years to allow the ordination of sexually active homosexual men and women, and to sanction active homosexual relationships by ordained clergy. This pressure, which has come from both within and without, has intensified since the 1991 publication of the report *Issues in Human Sexuality*, which allowed physical homosexual relationships for lay members of the Church of England, but prohibited them for clergy.[23]

Pressure from within the Church has taken various forms. Some bishops have broken ranks and have argued for the ordination of active homosexuals. One such is the retired Bishop of Salisbury, Dr John Austen Baker, who had great influence in writing *Issues in Human Sexuality*. His input was acknowledged by the Archbishop of Canterbury, who remarked that in formulating the report, 'we have been greatly helped by the work of a small group, chaired by the Bishop of Salisbury'.[24]

In April 1997 Dr Baker gave a lecture at St. Martin-in-the-Fields entitled *Homosexuality and Christian Ethics – a new way forward together*, in which he accepted homosexuality as 'a fact of human life',[25] and asked 'how do we use homosexuality to good and godly purpose?'[26] To reach this position Dr Baker abandoned all biblical laws on the issue. So far as the Old Testament is concerned, he commented that,

> 'biblical Judaism, through no fault of its own, could not conceive of homosexual orientation as part of a person's make-up. Such defects inevitably mean that the ethical commands in question lack authority, because the basis on which they were formulated was mistaken.'[27]

The New Testament teaching was never seriously considered. Instead the Bishop theorised that we 'need to take into account changed circumstances', [28] and that 'there are moral issues in many people's lives which cannot be resolved by universal rules.' [29]

Thus Dr Baker held that,

> 'erotic love can and often does have ... beneficial effects in the life of same-sex couples.' [30]

From this standpoint the Bishop argued logically for the ordination of sexually active homosexuals.

> 'I cannot see that married heterosexual clergy have a right to deny their homosexual brothers and sisters the potential spiritual blessing of a sexual relationship when they themselves enjoy that blessing ... If the church is willing to accept the ministry of homosexuals, then to impose on them a condition which most clergy are not prepared to undertake would seem to be unjust.' [31]

A growing number of bishops have taken a similar line. In 1997 the Bishop of Wolverhampton expressed his support for the ordination of active homosexuals, and paid tribute to other bishops who openly held the same view. [32]

Not all bishops are in favour of such a move, with the Archbishop of Canterbury, Dr Carey, and the retired bishop of Chester, Michael Baughen, being very much against. Nevertheless at the highest level the pressure is growing for a new Laodicean compromise.

The increasing number of clergy who are declaring themselves to be practising homosexuals has kept up the pressure for change. In a television interview in 1995 the Rt Rev. Derek Rawcliffe, a retired bishop, openly acknowledged his active homosexuality. Significantly, he remarked that 'he wanted to reassure priests who are gay that they are accepted by the church',[33] thus acknowledging that active homosexual clergy are already ministering in the Church.

It is impossible to say how many active homosexual clergy, both men and women, there are. Differing estimates have been made, often with a polemic intent. But the point is that some clergy who are known to be involved in homosexual relations are allowed to keep their posts and continue in their ministry.

Arguments have raged as to whether some bishops have knowingly ordained active homosexuals. Most bishops in England have denied so doing, although when Lord Runcie, the former Archbishop of Canterbury, was asked in a radio interview,

> 'Do you think – this may be an improper question – but have you knowingly ordained practising homosexuals?'

His reply was 'Yes', but he then qualified his answer by saying,

> 'I have not knowingly ordained anyone who told me they were a practising homosexual and were living in partnership with somebody as if it was a marriage.'[34]

Further pressure is being exercised by theological writers and various pro-homosexual groups, such as the Lesbian and Gay Christian Movement.

Despite such pressure from within the Church, of which the above is but a small sample, the Church of England has not taken the step of openly sanctioning the ordination of active homosexuals. Nevertheless the danger signals are all too apparent, and the pressure is mounting. We are following the well-worn steps of other major compromises.

This situation is not, of course, confined to the Church of England. Many bishops from the wider Anglican Communion are openly in favour of ordaining practising homosexuals. Some bishops of the Episcopal Church of the United States of America openly ordain active homosexuals. The Rt Rev. John Spong drew up a statement in 1994, calling for priestly ordination regardless of sexual orientation.[35] In 1996 an attempt to discipline a retired bishop, the Rt Rev. Walter Richter, for teaching that practising homosexuals could be ordained, and for ordaining an active homosexual, ended in failure. The bishops who examined the case decided, by a majority of seven to two, that neither the Church's doctrine nor its discipline, prohibited the ordination of practising homosexuals who were living in a stable relationship.[36]

Various churches in England are edging towards ordaining practising homosexuals. In 1994 the United Reformed Church accepted two openly homosexual people for ministerial training. One was in a longstanding relationship with a partner, and the other was open to such a relationship.[37] This led the 1997 General Assembly of the Church to consider the problem of the ordination of active gay or lesbian candidates. After debate the Assembly arrived at a classic Laodicean conclusion. It declared it was not in a position to come to a decision, and passed a resolution seeking 'further time and space to reflect on these matters.'[38] In the meantime local churches were allowed to refuse a minister on grounds of sexual activity, but the Assembly said it would also uphold a church which accepted a minister in an active homosexual relationship, subject to the approval of the local District Council.[39] The Assembly also stated that,

> 'the fact of a homosexual relationship shall not be the ground for rejecting a candidate for ministry during the process of selection, assessment, entry to a college or course and ministerial training.'[40]

As the Mission Council of the Church later admitted, this resolution 'committed the General Assembly to support a decision to ordain a person living in a homosexual relationship.'[41] No other Church in the United Kingdom had gone so far, and within the ranks of the United Reformed Church, 'some resigned their membership, others led their churches to consider secession, some ministers and their families felt betrayed and anxious about their future in a church which they now saw as having changed redically.'[42]

Such is the havoc caused by our Laodicean compromises.

References

1. 'The Ordering of Priests', *Book of Common Prayer*.
2. Richard Baxter, *The Reformed Pastor*, Banner of Truth Trust, 1983, p. 63.
3. Chapter 12 pp. 84–92.
4. Chapter 18 p. 151.
5. *The Canons of the Church of England*, Canon C4.3, 1969, p. 33. Extracts from 'The Canons of the Church of England' are copyright © The Central Board of Finance of the Church of England, 1969; The Archbishops' Council, 1999 and are reproduced by permission.
6. Chapter 13, references 17 and 25, p. 106.
7. *Marriage and the Church's Task*, p. 103.
8. *ibid.* p. 110.
9. *The Canons of the Church of England*, Canon C4.3, 1993, first supplement, 1994 p. 80. Extracts from 'The Canons of the Church of England' are copyright © The Central Board of Finance of the Church of England, 1993; The Archbishops' Council, 1999 and are reproduced by permission.
10. *Marriage and the Church's Task*, p. 107.
11. *ibid.* p. 105.
12. *ibid.* p. 105.
13. *ibid.* p. 111.
14. R. Hennessey, *The Breakdown of Clergy Marriages: A Discussion About and Research Into the Causes.* Crucible, October–December 1991, p. 201.
15. *ibid.* p. 202.
16. *Support for Clergy Marriage, A Consultation Paper by an Informal Working Party under the chairmanship of the Bishop of Winchester*, published by the Working Party, 1997, p. 1. Extracts from 'Support for Clergy Marriage' are copyright © The Central Board of Finance of the Church of England, 1997; The Archbishops' Council, 1999 and are reproduced by permission.
17. *Corporation of the Sons of the Clergy*, Report for the year 1996, p. 2.
18. *Support for Clergy Marriage*, p. 7.
19. *The Times* 25.10.1997.
20. *Church Times* 10.3.1995.
21. *Church Times* 7.3.1997.
22. P. Toon, *Are Modern Liberal Episcopalians Truly Liberal?* pp. 15, 16.
23. Chapter 15 pp. 122–124.
24. *Issues in Human Sexuality*, p. vii.
25. J.A. Baker, *Homosexuality and Christian Ethics – a new way forward together*, A lecture given at St Martin-in-the-Fields, April 1997, p. 10.
26. *ibid.* p. 10.
27. *ibid.* p. 7.
28. *ibid.* p. 7.

29. *ibid.* p. 8.
30. *ibid.* p. 11.
31. *ibid.* p. 13.
32. M. Bourke, Sermon preached at the 10th Anniversary Service of the Birmingham Branch of the Lesbian and Gay Christian Movement, 20.9.1997.
33. *Newsnight*, BBC2, 7.3.1995, reported in *Church Times* 10.3.1995.
34. *The Purple, the Blue and the Red*, BBC, Radio 4, 16.5.1996, reported in *Church Times* 17.5.1996.
35. *Church Times* 3.3.1995.
36. *Church Times* 24.5.1996.
37. *Human Sexuality Report 1999.* A Report of the Mission Council of the United Reformed Church. p. 3.
38. *Assembly Record*, United Reformed Church, 1997, Resolution 18 p. 11.
39. *ibid.* Resolution 19, p. 12.
40. *ibid.* p. 12.
41. *Human Sexuality Report 1999*, p. 5.
42. *ibid.* p. 5.

PART THREE

REPENTANCE

Chapter 22

Repentance

'Come, let us return to the Lord.'
(Hosea 6:1)

Compromise is essentially a spiritual problem. The Christian faith is not of this world. It was not devised by man, but revealed in all its perfection from God on high. The moment we try to change even the smallest part of what God has told us, we have entered a spiritual battle with God Himself. We are implying that we know better than He does, and have the power and authority to alter His ways according to our views.

Behind all our adjustments to the world lurks the devil, the father of lies. He knows that if God's people water down the truth, others will not find eternal life through Jesus, for a diluted faith has no power to save. At the same time Satan is aware that the more we bring God down to our level, the less we give Him glory and worship.

Compromise can only be fought by spiritual means. Human strength has no power in the spiritual realm. When our Lord spoke to the original Laodicean church, He told them in words of deepest love, *'be zealous and repent'* (Revelation 3:19). There was no other way.

We are the modern Laodicea. We are not simply **like** Laodicea of the first century. In a spiritual sense we **are** Laodicea. Therefore the message is exactly the same as of old. Be zealous and repent. This means repenting of our personal sins, and for the sins of the whole Church. We are to come before the Lord in deep love for His people, and in true contrition for our concessions to the spirit of the age.

Repentance is not a comfortable undemanding way. It is much easier to sit and grumble about the state of the Church, or sign petitions and pass resolutions which demand a return to biblical ways. But grumbling kills love, and no one is ever brought to repentance by a resolution. The 1998 Lambeth Conference declaration that homosexual behaviour was incompatible with Scripture,[1] welcome though it was, is a case in point. After the Conference an open letter of apology to homosexuals was signed by almost 200 bishops. Far from settling the controversy within the Anglican Church, the declaration helped to harden attitudes and deepen divisions.

Repentance is not easy because it involves throwing ourselves on God, and crying out to Him for mercy. There is that streak of rebellion lurking deep in the human spirit which does not like to admit of too much sin, and is repelled by the thought of trusting in God alone. We prefer to do things in our own strength. But the way of human endeavour is not open to us. We have to come before our loving God in personal humility and total self-abasement, with empty, dirty hands, pleading for His forgiveness, and trusting Him to cleanse us with the blood of Christ.

> 'Nothing in my hand I bring,
> Simply to Thy cross I cling.'[2]

There is no room for pride in repentance. We need to realise that we are at one in sin with the whole Body of Christ. This is far from easy. We much prefer to hide in little groups, and bask in pseudo-holy isolation. Yet every Christian is baptised into one body, and when one part sins the whole is affected. We cannot put our head in the sand. Neither can we say that our church or fellowship alone is walking in the truth. If the whole body is filled with cancer, even the little toe is affected.

True repentance involves a deep desire to amend our lives. It is not much use, for example, telling the Lord how sorry we are that the Church is unfaithful over money, if we do not show trust in our personal financial dealings.

Repentance means being willing to stand publicly against the tide of worldly compromise which is engulfing the western Church. There is little point in confessing the Church's laxity if we are not prepared to be open in our beliefs and act accordingly.

Therefore repentance entails suffering. We will suffer when the Holy Spirit shows us our personal failings. The weight of our sins will appal us, and we shall be crushed and humiliated before the Lord. In a similar fashion we shall suffer when we realise the great weight of the sins of the whole body. As the Holy Spirit opens our minds and hearts we shall feel despair and misery beyond human telling.

There will be suffering because the devil will try to prevent our repentance. He knows what it can achieve, and will use every trick to take even the idea from our minds. It is a general rule that the closer our prayer is to the mind of Christ, the harder the battle.

We will also suffer ridicule and calumny from the world, and even from within the Body of Christ. The world will regard us as mad, and those in the Church who see no need for repentance will mock and maybe reject us. But it is better to suffer for the sake of Christ, and to *'bear the abuse He endured'* (Hebrews 13:13), than to walk easily with the world.

Repentance, therefore, takes us to the foot of the cross, where we see the outpoured love of God for His world. There we see the Saviour suffering physical and spiritual agonies because of our sins. There we see blood and water pouring from His side, the blood that cleanses and the Holy Spirit that empowers His people. At the cross we see the total self-giving of the Son of God, and realise afresh our own total unworthiness.

If we are willing to say yes to God, and obey His command to repent, so we shall have the privilege of sharing a little in our Lord's agonies and spiritual sufferings.

We know that God loves His Church, and wants it cleansed, pure and spotless, *'prepared as a bride adorned for her husband'* (Revelation 21:2). We also know that *'if we confess our sins, He is faithful and just, and will forgive our sins and cleanse us from all unrighteousness'* (1 John 1:9). Our repentance, therefore, is a service of love to His Church, preparing the Bride for the great day.

Our Lord will always give us the strength to endure and overcome. If we obey His voice, and open the door, He will come to us and allow us to know the deep fellowship of His presence. And with Jesus with us, who or what can hurt us?

In the western world the Church of Jesus Christ lies wounded and bleeding. Are we willing to leave Laodicea, obey His call, and walk with Him, wherever He leads? He alone is the way to glory.

References

1. Chapter 15, p. 126.
2. A.M. Toplady, 'Rock of Ages', verse 3.

Postscript

This book was written before the atrocities of September 11th, 2001.

We are now coming face to face with the consequences of our deliberate rebellion against God and His ways, and who knows what further horrors lie ahead?

We desperately need clean hands to cope with this situation. If we are wrong with our God, then we have no power to overcome evil and deception in all its manifold forms. May this fact give us an added impetus as we consider our compromises with the Word of God.

Peter Noble
November 2001